Faith For All Generations

A FAMILY DEVOTIONAL

Robert Flood

Design and Illustrations by Keith R. Neely

Denver, Colorado 80215

A division of Accent Publications, Inc.
12100 W. Sixth Avenue
P.O. Box 15337
Denver, Colorado 80215

Printed in the United States of America

First published in 1984 under the title *Up With America*, ISBN 0-89636-128-4.
Library of Congress Catalog Card Number 84-70427

Library of Congress Catalog Card Number 86-70628
ISBN 0-89636-214-0

Contents

Preface

The American nation rests on a rich Biblical heritage, but today's subtle influence of secular humanism obscures it. ***Faith For All Generations*** rediscovers the America of today and yesteryear, while it explores the riches of Scripture at the same time. It is a devotional book with a fresh touch—designed both for the family and the classroom.

In its pages you will meet a great Pioneer scientist who started each day early with the Lord, and a Christian astronaut who has seen the "broad view" of the planet for which Jesus died.

Read the behind-the-scenes stories of the ***Star Spangled Banner*** and Pearl Harbor—and their Biblical applications.

Let the stories of the early-day circuit rider and the Pony Express give insight on how to share the gospel with others in your everyday world.

Meet historic American figures like Noah Webster, William Penn and George Washington Carver.

Learn about lighthouses, windmills and cable cars.

Follow the pioneers through the Cumberland Gap, and on westward over the rugged Oregon Trail.

Travel from lofty Pike's Peak to granite-faced Mount Rushmore and on to rumbling Mount St. Helens.

What lifted J.C. Penney from the depths of despair to merchandise fame? Why did the son of atheist Madalyn Murray O'Hair suddenly turn his life over to the same Lord he had once repudiated? This book will tell you.

Here is a blend of the past and the present that mixes history with modern times. A chronological chart of events is found at the back of the book.

So enjoy a spiritual uplift, linked with some fascinating Americana, as you sweep the centuries from Plymouth Rock to the space age.

1 American Jigsaw

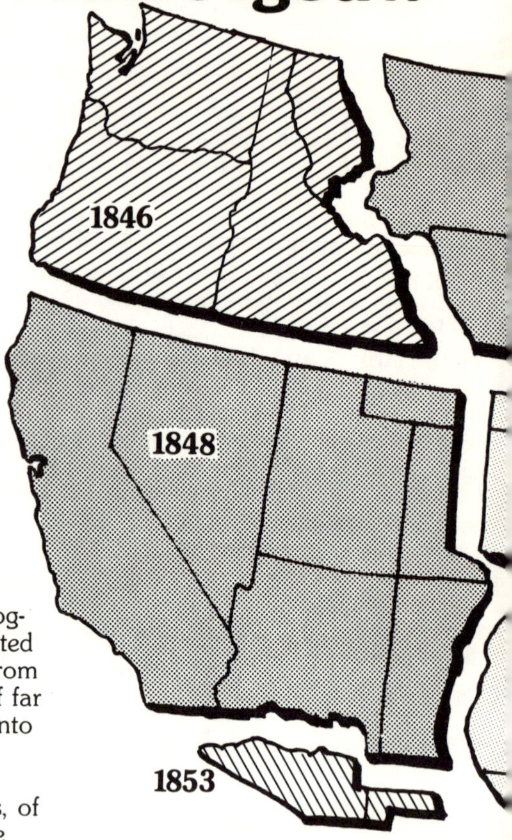

1846

1848

1853

The United States map as we know it today took shape piece by piece. So also God's plan for our lives unfolds one piece at a time.

Read: Ephesians 5:15-17

Almost any American can recognize immediately a map of the United States. Forty-eight states stretch from coast to coast. Alaska lies by itself far to the north, and Hawaii far out into the Pacific.

But it did not always look like this. The original thirteen colonies, of course, hugged the northeast. The treaty of 1783 with England that ended the Revolution granted the United States almost everything east to the Mississippi River.

But France still owned most of the Midwest. The United States picked this up in 1803 with the Louisiana Purchase, and more than doubled the size of the nation. It bought a small chunk of what is now North Dakota and Minnesota from the British in 1818, and purchased Florida from Spain in 1819, along with a piece of Louisiana.

Almost a half century passed before the United States enlarged its borders further. In 1845 it bought from the Spanish what is now much of Texas and New Mexico. The next year it acquired the Oregon Territory (which included Washington and Idaho). It picked up the Southwest, including California, from Mexico in 1848, then in 1853 added a little strip along the Mexican border called the Gadsden Purchase.

Did our forefathers fear for America's future?
How can you find God's plan for the future?

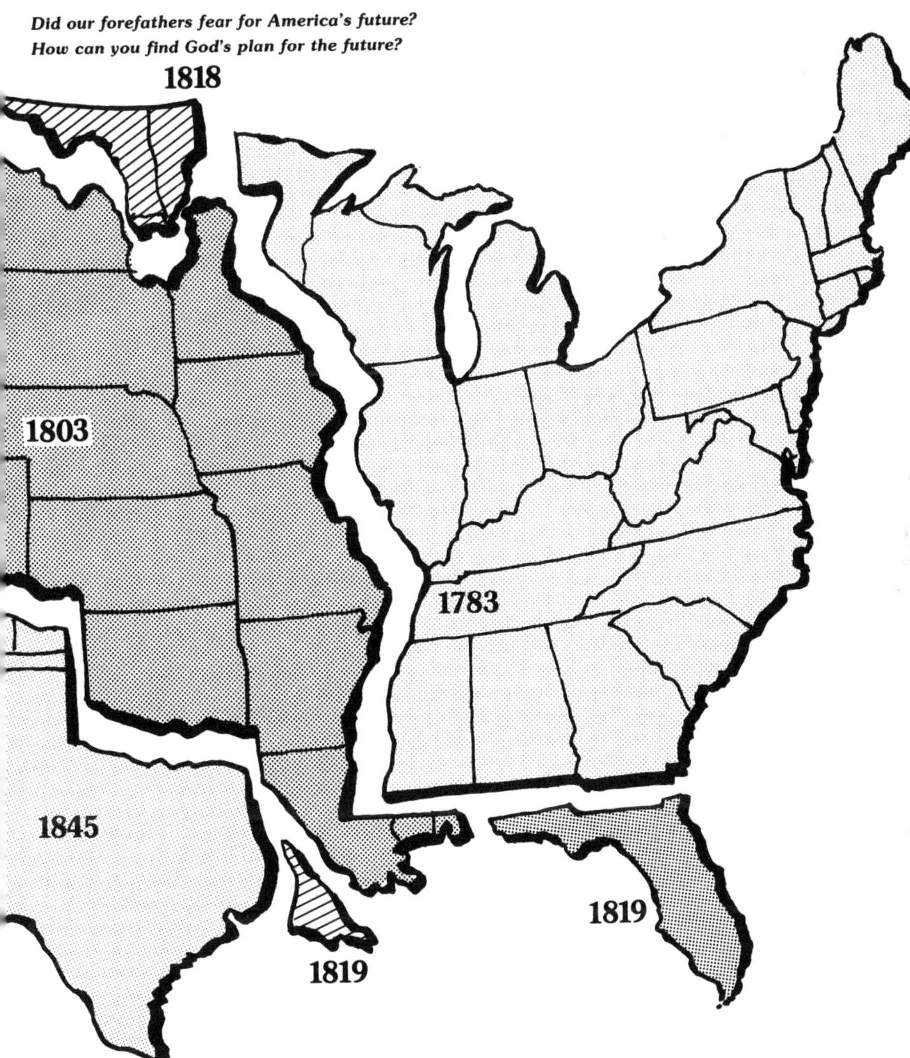

The territories of Alaska and Hawaii followed later.

Our forefathers could not have predicted the final shape of the Union. In colonial times it might well have appeared that the continent would be sliced up by Great Britain, France, Spain and Mexico. Call it a real jigsaw! Yet God knew all along what would eventually happen.

This is so also with your life. Who knows but God what final shape it will take? It would be so good, we think, if He would just lay out the whole plan for us, and let us see into the years ahead.

"Who will I marry?"

"Where will I live?"

"When will I die?"

"What, Lord, is really Your will for my life? Please lay out the map and let me see it."

God does show us His will for us, if we seek it. But not the whole plan at once. Instead, He unfolds it one segment at a time. Until the end, you are going to have to live with those "missing pieces."

In reality, your life unfolds only a day at a time. Each day has its unknown, and its opportunities. Each day gives you a fresh start. God says that His "mercies are new every morning." What then does God want you to do today? That is what counts the most.

Our passage in Ephesians says to be careful how you live (verse 15). Make the most of your time, and buy up the opportunities that come along (verse 16). "Don't act thoughtlessly, but try to find out and do whatever the Lord wants you to." Today.

Some people never get a good grip on "the will of the Lord" because, to them, it is always something in the future. God is most concerned about what you do today. But don't wait for a printed telegram from God to fall from the sky. Simply keep digging into the Word of God, bit by bit. And keep moving. God's will often unfolds only after you move into action.

Avoid what you know is wrong. You'll probably soon begin to discover "what the will of the Lord is."

Then someday you and God, who "knows the end from the beginning," will see all the pieces in place.

The Russians were Here!

It may surprise many Americans to know that as late as the presidency of John Tyler, the Russians held a toehold of the continental United States!

In 1812 ninety-five Russian fur traders and some native Alaskans quietly established Fort Ross, along the foggy coastline north of San Francisco, while the other major European powers were preoccupied with other concerns. Though intrigued with territorial expansion, Russia finally withdrew in 1841, only a few years before California was ushered into the Union.

The replica of an old Russian Orthodox chapel still stands at Fort Ross. It reminds us that, except for the providence of God, Russia may have eventually staked claim to much of the West!

U.S. Postage Stamps commemorate the acquisition of the Oregon Territory, and the Gadsden purchase.

2 "What Hath God Wrought!"

Samuel F. B. Morse.

Is it possible for man to create?

Does your life confess of God's existence?

When Samuel F. B. Morse sent his historic telegraph message from Washington D.C. to Baltimore, he knew that man's scientific discoveries never catch God by surprise.

Read: Job 37:14-24

On a hot summer day in 1844, Samuel F. B. Morse clicked an historic message from Washington D.C. to Baltimore over the telegraph system he had invented. Using the code of dots and dashes, or short and long clicks, that he had devised, he dispatched this brief message:

"What hath God wrought!"

Morse had invented the system twelve years before, but it took him more than a decade to get it recognized. Surely he deserved great tribute, and he got it. The telegraph made Morse a famous and wealthy man.

Yet the message Morse chose to send on that day did not call attention to himself. Instead, it pointed to God. Morse understood clearly that all our scientific achievements and discoveries, in the final analysis, point not to man, but to God.

Such is the thrust of Job 37. Though written long before our modern scientific era, its truths are eternal. The wonders of God's creation surround us. Elihu, in his debate with Job, refers to them as "the wondrous works of God." Scientific knowledge can easily impress us. But behind it all, we ought to be impressed, most of all, with God.

What is the logic?

God created all things. The Scriptures make this clear, and what we see around us shouts the same truth, in spite of evolution's popularity in our day. Therefore, when man "creates," he merely unfolds or harnesses what already exists. God, on the other hand, created out of nothing (ex nihilo)!

Samuel Morse's telegraph showed genius, but he knew he was only orchestrating the scientific dynamics that were already there.

When Wilbur and Orville Wright lifted their flying machine into the air at Kitty Hawk, North Carolina, on that historic day in 1903, the world knew they had solved at last the mystery of flight that had baffled mankind down through the ages.

But the Wright Brothers were quick to realize that they had simply discovered some "secrets" of the world around them that God had known all along. Said one of the men to the other after their success:

"And to think it was there all the time!"

No scientific discovery ever catches God by surprise.

Job 37 walks the reader through the mysteries of thunder, snow, rain and other weather phenomena (verses 10-13). It then considers lightning, the clouds, the winds (verses 14-18), and the brightness of the sun (verse 22). Yet God's brilliance and majesty are far greater, and His wisdom is far beyond ours. "No wonder men everywhere fear Him!" says the closing verse."For He is not impressed by the world's wisest men!"

The New Testament makes clear that God the Son shares this wisdom.

In Jesus Christ are hid "all the treasures of wisdom and knowledge" (Colossians 2:3). Our Lord knows

U.S. Postage Stamp of Samuel F. B. Morse.

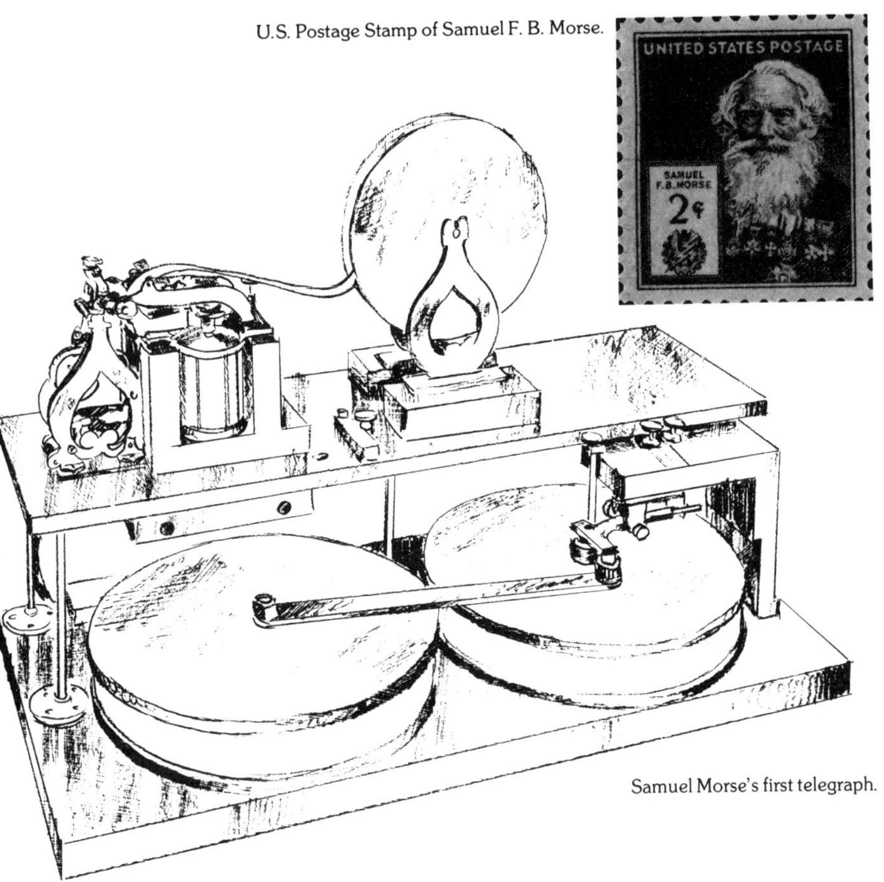

Samuel Morse's first telegraph.

every part of the universe, and understands every mystery of science.

The Morse Family

Samuel Morse found it easy to talk about God. His father, the Rev. Jedidiah Morse, was known as one of the strongest and most outspoken Christians of his day. And he was not just a preacher. He wrote the first geography book published in the United States and thereby became known as the "father of American geography."

Jedidiah Morse was also one of the first Americans to publish his religious views in tracts, and he spent his final years as a missionary to the Indians.

His son, Samuel, though most famous for his invention of the telegraph, had multiple talents. He earned fame as an accomplished artist before he was ever an inventor. His work "The Gallery of the Louvre" was sold in 1982 for three and a quarter million dollars—the most ever paid for an American painting!

3

Does God give power for Christian living? How? Are you choosing His power?

The Cable Car: Hang On!

The San Francisco cable car must cling to its power source to move ahead. Christians also must know how to hold fast, and not let go.

Read: I Thessalonians 5:15-22

The city of San Francisco lies almost entirely on hills, and its downtown buildings are on some of the steepest. It is little surprise then that early in the town's history someone had to come up with a rather ingenius invention to conquer these slopes: the cable car.

Give the credit to Andrew S. Hallidie, who had made his start by designing and building ore cableways for gold mines. He simply adapted its principles to create a cable railroad.

His first San Francisco cable railroad began operation in August,

1873. The line was a little more than a half-mile long with a climb of 307 feet.

How does the cable car work? You might be surprised to realize it has no power of its own. Its secret is the cable hidden underneath the street pavement, in a slot between the tracks. The cable moves continuously, activated by a central power station somewhere along the route. Each cable car has a grip device that extends through a slot to the moving cable beneath. To move forward the operator must engage this grip to the cable. To stop he disengages the cable, and applies the brakes.

The Christian, like the cable car, has no real power apart from his Power Source. That power is Jesus Christ. Let go of the Lord, try to go it on your own, and somehow the forward momentum seems to grind to a standstill.

Some time ago the power station that ran the San Francisco cable car system had to be shut down for major repairs. The cable cars stood idle for months. Thousands of residents, and tourists alike, could not ride them, and tourism suffered. That's what happens when the power is cut.

There are things in life that the Christian must hold on to. First Thessalonians 5 tells us to "hold fast" to that which is good (verse 21).

A U.S. Postage Stamp pays tribute to the historic cable car.

We must also "hold fast" to sound doctrine. Timothy says to "hold fast the form of sound words, which thou hast heard of me in faith and love which is in Christ Jesus" (II Timothy 1:13). To put it another way, "don't let go of the Scriptures." It's a sure way to head off on the wrong track.

We are also to "hold fast" our profession of Jesus Christ (see Hebrews 4:14). Guard your testimony. Don't let it get away. Keep on trusting in the Lord. Hang on.

The Old Testament, too, reminds us to maintain our grip. "You are to cling to the Lord your God," we read, "as you have done unto this day" (Joshua 23:8).

There's another truth about cable cars. When the operator releases the grip from the cable, he had better also apply the brakes without delay. A cable car with no brakes—and it has happened at least a time or two—is headed for disaster. So are Christians who let go of the Lord, and then ignore the brakes that would keep them from being at the mercy of all the forces around them ready to pull them down.

Turn-Around

The cable car has no reverse. At the end of each line is a turntable. The operator simply positions his car on the turntable and looks for his passengers, and any bystanders, to help turn him around.

By 1877 cable cars of one type or another operated in twenty American cities, and also in several foreign countries. By the end of the 19th Century, however, the development of practical electric power led to their decline.

4

Does God see things differently than we do?

Can you understand things from another's point of view? from God's?

An Astronaut's View and God's View

Whatever the circumstances on planet Earth, or the turmoil of the moment in your own life, our Saviour never loses His world view.

Read: John 3:16-21

It was July 30, 1971, little more than a decade ago, when Apollo 15 hit the moon with jolting impact. Astronauts Jim Irwin and David Scott lunged in their lunar module as it pitched and tilted dangerously on the rim of a small crater.

For a frightening moment it appeared that the men might have to abort their mission—or be left stranded on the moon, without hope of rescue. The astronauts froze in position while Mission Control in Houston, nearly one quarter million miles away, monitored all systems for possible damage from the hard landing. The order came back for them to "stay." The men powered down, pounded each other on the shoulder, and peered out.

They looked across a beautiful valley with high mountains on three sides and the deep gorge of Hadley Rille a mile to the west.

Irwin and Scott spent three days and nights on the moon. Often they looked up to see the earth hanging in space—with its hues of blue and brown and green and white. "When you see the earth from space," says Irwin, "you don't see any evidence of man's existence at all. All you can

see is the beauty of the land and the water."

"I lifted up my hand at arm's length," he says, "and blotted out the entire earth—all that I had ever known."

Yet in this unbelievably remote setting, Irwin experienced "an overwhelming sense of the presence of God."

Most likely none of us will ever have the privilege of seeing firsthand the entire earth from the moon's vantage point.

It's too bad. It would probably revolutionize our lives.

As Christians we sometimes have such a pathetically small view—of the world around us, of our mission, of the church, of God. Seldom do men take the time to step back and look at the whole.

But God looks at the whole.

Note today's familiar passage. God loved the world. Not just a piece of it. Not just one nation, one denomination, one social class, one nationality.

God sent His Son into the world. Not just into Bethlehem or Jerusalem. He said He came not to condemn the world, but to save it. The entire world—if men would only respond.

"Light has come into the world," John says. Later in the same Gospel Jesus clarifies the analogy. "I am the Light of the world," He says (see John 8:12).

Even the sun can shine on only half of the earth at one time, while the other side lies in darkness. The astronauts could see only one side. And even on the lighted side, they could see no people.

But God sees all, and knows every life, every heart, every thought. The clouds of failure or personal hurt cannot blot out God's light—not even in one's deepest distress.

God cares and understands. Remember, God sent His Son to dwell among us on planet Earth. Later He arose from the dead and returned to His Father's presence.

Our Saviour, who with the Father created our very universe, never loses His world view.

James Irwin and the lunar roving vehicle.

This Apollo 8 Postage Stamp reminds us that God is Creator.

Astronauts and God

When astronaut James Irwin returned from his Apollo 15 mission, the former test pilot decided he wanted to do more with his life than fly. It was more important, he felt, to tell others of the Saviour's love. Irwin formed a Christian organization called High Flight, based in Colorado Springs, and for the past decade has been preaching the gospel across the United States and around the world. "God walking on earth," he says, "is more important than man walking on the moon."

On Christmas eve in 1968, Apollo 8 astronauts read from the opening chapter of Genesis as their spacecraft orbited the moon. Can you name the three astronauts on that flight? (Answer: Frank Borman, William Anders and James Lovell).

Astronaut Jack Lousma, who commanded the March 1982 flight of the space shuttle **Columbia**, relied heavily on complex computer guidance to bring his craft into a pinpoint landing in New Mexico. Lousma says the best guidance for young people, however, is Proverbs 3:5-6.

Can you find at least one verse in the Old Testament and one verse in the New Testament about the moon? (Suggestions: Try Psalm 8:3 and Acts 2:20.)

Suggestion

If the moon is out tonight, why not go outside after dark to see it.

Does God care about the laws of America? Would you be willing to move in order to worship God?

Our Pilgrim Heritage

When the Mayflower landed at Plymouth Rock, Christian settlers laid the foundations for a republic that would endure through the centuries.

Read:
I Corinthians 3:10-11

When Americans look back to their beginnings, they usually point to the little band of sea-weary pioneers that landed in 1620 at Plymouth Rock. Of the more than one hundred pilgrims aboard the Mayflower, the majority were devout Christians. They were Separatists bent on shaking the Church of England and building a new life in an unknown wilderness, where they could worship the Lord in the way they believed the Scriptures taught.

When these pilgrims drew up the Mayflower Compact, they laid the

The Mayflower.

foundations of law and order and established the first "civil body politic" in America.

They could not have foreseen, of course, any long-range significance at the time. The Mayflower Compact was intended only as a temporary pact to keep law and order among themselves in a wilderness where there was no law.

At the heart of the compact lay an undisputed conviction that God must be at the center of all law and order and that law without a moral base is really no law at all.

The compact also rested on a "covenant" agreement, and this would later help lay the foundations of the American republic. All law, they insisted, would rest not upon a monarchy or a dictatorship, but upon "the consent of the governed."

This is why, today, the inscription on the Plymouth Rock monument reads:

> ***They laid the foundation of a state wherein every man through countless ages should have liberty.***

It is so important to lay the right foundation. Lay the foundation crooked, and the whole building will be crooked. Build a weak foundation, and the superstructure upon it will eventually collapse.

The Apostle Paul did his best to lay the right foundations. In I Corinthians 3 he gives all credit for his expertise as a "builder" to God (verse 10). He also credits his associate, Apollos, who had built upon his work. But now he warns all those who would build thereafter. Christians down through the ages, he implies, will build with different materials, different methods, even different theologies. In the final analysis, God will judge what they build, and whether it has lasting value.

Jesus Christ, he warns, is the only foundation upon which man can successfully build (verse 11)—either the church or his individual life.

It is so easy to build our lives on the wrong foundations: selfish ambition, material success, pleasure. Many do not realize the faulty base upon which they've built, until perhaps years later when the structure collapses, or they stand off far enough to see clearly what they've really constructed.

Tragically, wrong foundations shortchange generations to come. Spiritual neglect shows up in our children, and in their children's children.

Be careful what foundations you lay.

Private Enterprise

It has been said that the Pilgrims, by example, laid the first foundations for American private enterprise. But they learned the hard way.

By arrangement with those back in England who had financed their venture, the settlers at first ran a "collective" farm operation. Before long, though, they observed that the socialistic approach had squelched incentive, bred confusion and discontent and retarded "much employment that would have been to their benefits and comforts." So they soon discarded the system for private enterprise.

Production spiraled, the Pilgrims prospered, and they eventually more than paid off their investors back home.

Does the Lord warn men of danger?
How has He protected you?

Lighthouses on the Sea

Along the coasts of America they warn mariners of dangerous shoals. On the seas of life, man needs to see Light in the darkness.

Read: John 1:1-9

Maine lighthouse on U.S. Postage Stamp.

They call it the Boston Light, and it was erected by the Massachusetts Bay Colony on Little Brewster Island off the entrance to Boston Harbor in 1716. It became the first lighthouse in the United States. Today there are no less than ten thousand lighthouses, all operated by the United States Coast Guard.

The nation's tallest lighthouse can be found at Cape Hatteras, North Carolina. Visitors climb 275 steps to its balcony.

Some lighthouse beams are extremely powerful and can be seen as far away as sixty-five miles. Their range is reduced, of course, by such factors as fog, rain, snow, haze and smoke. The higher the light above the water, the farther it can be seen. Lights can be white, red, green, or another color. They can burn steadily, flash slowly, or flash quickly—as many as sixty flashes per second.

It is important that a lighthouse be painted a color that makes it stand out from its backdrop. Offshore lighthouses are usually painted red, with white lettering.

Whatever the specifics, lighthouses are built to shine in the darkness and let seamen know the right course to take.

When Jesus Christ came down to planet Earth, He brought light to men. The opening verses of John's Gospel describe Him as "light in the darkness." It was so bright, that the darkness could never extinguish it. Unlike even the most powerful lighthouse, whose light eventually fades in the distance, this Light could not be overcome.

A lighthouse beam disappears once a ship is over the curve of the horizon and no longer in its direct sight. Jesus Christ, however, describes Himself as "the light of the world: he that followeth me shall not walk in darkness, but shall have the light of life" (John 8:12).

Lighthouse at Portland Head, Maine.

There is no greater contrast than darkness and light. Most lights seem almost useless in the daytime, at least outside on a bright sunny day. But as twilight approaches and darkness moves in, the lights of a city, for instance, take on clear, bright image against the blackening sky.

It may seem at times like the darkness of sin in the world will surely overcome us. Yet the darker the backdrop, the more the message of the gospel seems to stand out. It is true also of vibrant Christians. They tend to stand out all the more against the backdrop of a decadent society. The Apostle Paul once wrote, "where sin abounded, grace did much more abound" (Romans 5:20).

Darkness cannot overcome us. Jesus is the Light. Satan would like to snuff out that Light and send men crashing into treacherous shoals to their own destruction. He cannot destroy the Light, but he can persuade people to ignore it.

This is the greatest peril upon life's sea.

Hymns of the Sea

There are numerous hymns of the Christian faith which take their analogies from the sea. How many can you name?

(Partial answer: "Jesus, Saviour, Pilot Me," "Will Your Anchor Hold in the Storms of Life?", "Let the Lower Lights Be Burning.")

Suggestion: Read a stanza of one of these hymns, and compare it to the Christian way of life.

7

Can someone tell if your faith is real?
How is God real in your life?

Go and Tell

The early frontier circuit rider knew that in order to spread the gospel far and wide, he had to go where the people were.

Read: Mark 5:2-20

Names like Davy Crockett and Daniel Boone still live on as great legends of the American frontier. They were rugged men who knew how to survive in the wilderness. Just as remarkable, though, were some of America's early-day circuit riders.

These were preachers on horseback, who roamed the wilderness in all kinds of weather to search out pioneers who needed to hear the gospel and Christians who needed encouragement. Though people were hidden in the wilderness, they missed few cabins.

Methodists took the initiative with the circuit rider concept. Probably the most amazing of them all was Francis Asbury. In the early 1800s, when thousands of pioneers left their homes and churches in the East and trekked through the Cumberland Gap into the forests beyond, Asbury went after them. He was determined to bring Jesus to them where they were.

Despite the peril of Indian attacks, the cold of winter, and the absence of roads, Asbury roamed the American wilderness for forty years. He planted the seeds of the gospel everywhere, like a spiritual Johnny Appleseed, and then came back year after year to examine the harvest.

It is said that Francis Asbury may have traveled more than one quarter million miles. And he preached some twenty-five thousand sermons!

Before the Revolutionary War, the Anglican church and the Congregationalists had dominated American Protestantism. But they weren't prepared for the great migration West. The Anglicans, in particular, were content to remain entrenched in their churches along the Eastern seaboard. The Methodists, still rather obscure on the American religious scene, sent out circuit riders. The Baptists sent their "farmer-preachers." A half century later, these two groups had surged far ahead.

The basic message of today's Scripture text is simple: "Go and tell what great things he hath done for thee." (See Mark 5:19,20.)

This is not the spirit of much of today's evangelicalism. Instead, the motto seems to be, "If they come to me, I'll tell them." Or, "if they'll just

Circuit rider Francis Asbury at the Cumberland Gap.

walk in the front door of my church, they'll hear the gospel."

It has been said that "if you want to fish, you have to go where the fish are."

Some of today's younger Christians, in particular, have caught the "go and tell" spirit. Christian groups swarm to the Florida beaches at Easter to tell the crowds there about Jesus. Some venture into the city ghettos, or the teenage hangouts, or the hills of Appalachia.

Most of the men and women, boys and girls, who need Jesus are seldom or never in church. They're in their homes down the street, in the shopping malls, in restaurants, at sports events.

The frontier Baptist preacher had the right idea also. He moved with the people, lived among them, farmed alongside of them, and tried to help his brother at every turn. He also shared the gospel. They knew he was "one of them."

Some of today's most dynamic evangelism is of this kind. Truckers are reaching truckers. Lawyers are reaching lawyers. Businessmen are winning other businessmen, airline pilots other pilots, students other students. That's the old farmer-preacher concept.

Perhaps we need more of the early pioneer spirit.

"Go and tell what great things He hath done for thee."

Christian airline personnel reach out to their fellow workers through breakfasts, luncheons, banquets, book-racks, Bible study groups and one-to-one witness. They hold an annual convention, or retreat, atop Lookout Mountain, Tennessee.

The Christian Legal Society is one of the fastest-growing evangelical movements in the country. It reaches out to other lawyers, attorneys, judges and law school students. Chapters now exist in most of the nation's law schools.

Several Christian groups minister to truckers. Mobile truck chapels crisscross the nation, holding safety lectures at truck terminals—and presenting the gospel. Some major truckstops now have their own chaplains.

The Nurses Christian Fellowship, an arm of the Inter-Varsity movement, has been spreading the gospel in these ranks now for more than forty years.

The Christian Medical Society, whose board has even included the Surgeon General, continues to send millions of dollars worth of donated pharmaceutical drugs and medical equipment annually to countries around the world.

In the West, rodeo cowboys are spreading the gospel among other cowboys, and among ranchers as well. Since 1973 they have distributed more than sixty thousand copies of the "Cowboy Bible."

Reaching Out

Job or occupation has proved to be the common ground for some of today's most dynamic evangelism. Here are a few examples:

Suggestion:

Ask the Lord to give you one person that you will try to reach with the gospel in the next twelve months.

Is our prosperity important to the Lord? What things are valuable to you?

The Gold Rush: It's Still On

Early day crowds streamed West to strike it rich. But God tells us that our Christian faith is more precious than gold.

Read: I Peter 1:3-7

In 1848 the sleepy town of San Francisco consisted of about five hundred people. Then one day a man rushed into town shouting "Gold! Gold from the American River!" The word spread like wildfire. People from the East headed West in covered wagons labeled "California or Bust!" Gold-seekers poured in from as far away as Australia, all with dreams of making it big overnight. San Francisco and mountain towns in the Sierras boomed.

Gold and silver—tons of it—brought settlers flocking to Colorado in the mid-and-late 1800s. These were wild times in places like Denver, Aspen, Leadville, and Central City. One undertaker even advertised group-rate burials for Saturday killings!

Miners went after their gold with pans and picks and shovels. At first it was plainly visible. But those deposits have long since played out. Today scientists and technicians hunt "invisible" gold—gold so fine and scattered that it can be found only with super-powerful electron microscopes. These firms must process a pile of ore as big as a house to get even a pound of gold.

Gold and silver once brought miners, gamblers and gunmen to Nevada, where the fabulous Comstock Lode yielded more than a billion dollars. But the precious metals finally gave out. Today nearly two hundred ghost towns dot the Nevada landscape, their weather-worn buildings deserted and creaking in the wind. Most were once thriving mining camps, where thousands sought sudden wealth.

A few found that wealth, but most didn't. And even many of those

Pan for gold attraction, Knott's Berry Farm, California.

U.S. Postage Stamps recall the early-day gold and silver booms.

who did quickly squandered it away, until once more they had nothing.

That's the way many people are with sudden wealth. They don't know how to handle prosperity. They're unhappy without wealth, yet often also miserable with it, because they have totally twisted or ignored the true values of life. The Apostle Paul, on the other hand, knew how to live happily whether he had much or little (see Philippians 4:11). That's because he had his values in the right place.

First Peter 1 lays the gift of eternal life alongside all other possessions and calls it "priceless." Yet the privilege of knowing Jesus Christ in this life, and the blessing that lies yet beyond, have no price tag. They are free for the asking, because Jesus Christ died and rose again. He has already paid the price—for the richest commodity we could ever hope to own.

Today's passage in I Peter says that even those trials which sometimes test our faith also have great value. They are, to God, more precious than gold. No one can steal from you the riches you have in Jesus Christ. They will never decay. Psalm 49 makes clear that when man dies, he takes no earthly wealth with him. It stays behind. The government may take much of it. Those who inherit it often squander it, or squabble over it.

The fight over possessions, it seems, will help trigger the great battle in the Middle East, as recorded in Ezekiel 38:13.

Not long ago, when the gold market soared, people rushed after it. In other months they chased after silver. Yet Proverbs 16:16 says, "How much better is it to get wisdom than gold! and to get understanding rather to be chosen than silver!" Such wisdom comes from the Scriptures, and is found by those who seek God.

A good reputation, also, is more valuable than gold. Solomon says, "A good name is rather to be chosen than great riches, and loving favour rather than silver and gold" (Proverbs 22:1).

So often man looks in the wrong place when he wants to strike it rich!

Quiz

In what state will you find:
The largest gold mine? (South Dakota —the Homestead Mine in Lead.)
The largest silver mine? (Idaho—the Sunshine Mine near Kellogg.)
The largest copper mine? (Utah—the Kennicott mine west of Salt Lake City, largest open-pit copper mine in North America.)

Can God's priorities make our lives more productive?
Do you start each day with God?

Orders for the Day

Scientist, artist, musician, agriculturalist—George Washington Carver was all four. How was he able to accomplish so much?

Read: Psalm 92:1-2

Henry Ford once called George Washington Carver "the world's greatest living scientist." It may have been a slight overstatement, although considering the odds against him, Carver's life was little short of miraculous.

He was born a slave in 1864, then orphaned as a child. His health was poor. Everything seemed stacked against him. But at an early age he came to know Jesus as his Saviour. His spiritual life grew and always remained in the heart of his priorities.

George Washington Carver, agricultural scientist.

Carver was the first black man to study at Iowa State, where he earned highest honors and a master's degree. He also turned down an offer to teach there. Instead, he answered a call to serve his people at Alabama's Tuskegee Institute.

There Carver not only taught the South how to grow peanuts, but also what to do with them. He discovered more than three hundred products that could be made from peanuts—everything from "coffee" to sand and feathers! Carver found not only hundreds of uses for peanuts, but also for sweet potatoes and soybeans.

His fame in agricultural chemistry grew, but Carver had other talents as well. He was also an artist and musician.

Near the close of his life, he made an appearance before the Congress of the United States. At one point, members of Congress asked him how he had managed to accomplish so much in his lifetime.

After a moment's pause, he replied, "At four o'clock each morning I sit down and ask the Creator what I am to do that day. Then I go ahead and do it."

The one who can climb out of bed at four o'clock in the morning for his quiet time would have to be the exception.

Yet the Scriptures say a great deal about the start of a new day. The opening verses of Psalm 92 remind us to thank Him early in the day. It is a good habit, because it helps to establish the tone of the day, and to set priorities. Each day of life is a gift from our Lord and offers its own fresh start.

"His mercies are new every morning." (See Lamentations 3:22,23.)

At the end of the day, says Psalm 92, look back upon its events and thank the Lord for His faithfulness. Let thanks become a habit, an attitude, and somehow the burdens of the day will fade.

"From the rising of the sun to the going down of the same, the Lord's name is to be praised" (Psalm 113:3).

But does the busy man or woman really have time to pray? The activist too often says no. "I've got to hit my list of things to do." Yet somehow that person never really gets on top, and wasted motion of one kind or another seems to eat up so much time.

George Washington Carver saw it another way. He was too busy **not** to let God set his priorities for the day. And that's probably why he accomplished so much.

To perceive God's orders, one must listen. It is easiest to hear in silence, but often silence can be found only in those early morning hours.

It's one thing, of course, to hear the voice of the Lord, and another to act decisively upon it. The words of Mary to the servants at the marriage in Cana, may say it best: "Whatsoever he saith unto you, do it" (John 2:5).

What great potential if all Christians, like Carver, could rise early and seek their orders.

The Amazing Carver

George Washington Carver made more than 300 products from the peanut, among them were instant "coffee," soap and ink.

He developed more than 100 products from the sweet potato, including flour, shoe blacking and candy.

He made synthetic marble from wood shavings; dyes from clay; and starch, gum and wallboard from cotton stalks.

10

Can God be honored by man's success? How? What things do you do best?

Noah Webster: Even Great Men Need Jesus

Some people are so nice. Some have done so much good for those around them. Yet can it really be true that they, too, may need to be saved?

Read: Romans 3:23; II Timothy 1:12

Noah Webster. Though he lived some two centuries ago, we still know his name well. The name Webster has endured, partly because millions of Americans today still use a Webster's dictionary. Of course, it has been updated many times over the years.

This great man was also a lawyer. He launched a daily newspaper in New York and helped to establish Amherst College. And he routinely rubbed shoulders with men like George Washington, Alexander Hamilton and John Jay. But, above all other accomplishments, it was his spelling book and his dictionary that made him so famous.

No man was more honest, or more revered, than was Noah Webster. Webster respected religion, and he had absorbed many Christian values. Surely then this man, in the thinking of many around him, would merit a place in Heaven.

But at the age of forty Noah Webster himself began to have some doubts. Maybe, he decided, he was resting his religious beliefs more on his own accomplishments than on the simple grace of God. It hurt his pride to admit this, but just maybe it was true.

So Noah Webster began to dig into the Bible to see exactly what it had to say. In time his objections to the simple gospel crumbled, one by one. One evening he fell to his knees, confessed his sins,and implored pardon through the merits of Jesus alone. For the first time he understood clearly that salvation always rests on the work God has done, not on the work that man has done.

Noah Webster.

The next morning he called his family together. With deep emotion he told them of his decision the night before. He also apologized that for years he had neglected his role as a spiritual leader in the home.

Noah Webster made a public profession of his faith in April, 1808. Three daughters soon followed with decisions of their own.

Webster continued in his daily study of the Scriptures over the years, despite the demands on his time in completing the **American Dictionary** (as it was called then). Certain definitions in those earlier editions clearly reflect his Christian stance.

All men, despite their best efforts, fall far short of salvation, apart from

Jesus Christ. Jesus came down to planet Earth, died and rose again to rescue us from an impossible situation. We are saved not according to our good works (all the good we may have done), but by pure grace. That is why no one can boast about his salvation. He can only lift up the Lord.

Yet non-believers sometimes tab Christians as "self-righteous." In actuality, the self-righteous person is the one who says he can make it on his own—without Jesus.

Though having all the qualities that might have made him "righteous" in the eyes of men, Noah Webster was not ashamed to invite the Saviour into his life in the midstream of his career.

The tall, slender Webster walked with a light and elastic step until the time of his death at age eighty-five. As he faced the close of his life on earth, the records say he quoted to a friend the very words that close today's Scripture passage:

"I know whom I have believed, and am persuaded that he is able to keep that which I have committed unto him against that day" (II Timothy 1:12).

Even great men need Jesus.

Before You Start . . .

If you happen to have a Webster's Dictionary in your home, bring it to the table as you begin family devotions.

Closing Tip

Read about Noah Webster in the encyclopedia. What other contributions to America did he make? How many of your friends and relatives know that Webster was a Christian?

More Insights on Noah Webster

Like a computer, Webster systematized his mind into huge files of knowledge. When he began to study the Bible in the midstream of life, he tackled its contents with the same kind of meticulous care that had characterized his work on **The American Dictionary.**

What made Webster's dictionary so significant at the time? It was the first dictionary published in America. Until its release in 1828 colonialists had to rely on British dictionaries, whose spelling and meanings did not reflect the changes of a pioneer setting upon the English language.

At one point in his language pursuits, Webster diverted from his labors on defining words to trace the origin of the English language and its connection with those of other countries. After researching the vocabularies of twenty of the principal languages of the world, he sharply opposed the evolutionary concept that insisted that language had emerged with the progressive development of animal life from "grunts to groans."

It took Noah Webster at least eighteen years (some records suggest even a longer period) to complete his dictionary. The day he finished the job, Noah Webster and his wife kneeled in prayer to thank the Lord for seeing them through such a gigantic task.

Footnote:

Noah Webster is not to be confused with Daniel Webster, a great early American statesman. The two Websters were contemporaries.

11

Is it important to know when you need help?
Do you follow the authority of others?

The Oregon Trail

Early pioneers, headed for the Northwest, chose a good trail boss and relied on those who had already scouted the route. Who will you follow into the unknown?

Read: Psalm 25:4-12

On the banks of the Mississippi River at St. Louis, Missouri, a huge Gateway Arch soars into the sky, framing the city's skyline from miles away. St. Louis used to be "where the West begins," and this monument celebrates the trek of some 300,000 men, women and children in history's greatest overland migration: The Oregon Trail.

The historic trail began here, where pioneers loaded their covered wagons, chose a trail boss and headed out across two thousand miles of mud and dust, mountain and plain.

A typical train consisted of fifty or more wagons, each covered by canvas or other waterproof material. The Oregon Trail followed the Platte and North Platte rivers westward, crossing the Rockies over South Pass. It then shifted slightly southward to Fort Bridger, where in the earlier days of the migration wagons were exchanged for pack horses, and the journey continued along the Snake and Columbia rivers.

Some points on the trail proved a brutal test of both wagon and stock. After the descent of Windlass Hill, a wagon inevitably would need repair. There the pioneers eased wagons down not with a winch, but with a prayer and a scheme: "We detach all the oxen from the wagon except the wheel yoke, lock the two hind wheels"—and hitch oxen to the rear, to pull against gravity, along with a dozen men holding ropes taut.

Many born-again Christians were among those whose wagons etched the 2,000-mile Oregon Trail into the American landscape. As early as 1834, before there was barely a trail, Methodist missionary Jason Lee and his associates had taken the gospel into Oregon's fertile Willamette Valley.

Those who traveled the Oregon Trail put a great deal of trust in their guides, or trail bosses. And they relied heavily on those who had already been over the trail before.

The heart of Psalm 25 is a prayer for guidance. "Show me thy ways, O Lord; teach me thy paths" (verse 4).

From Genesis to Revelation, the Lord can be seen as our Supreme Guide. God marked the trail of life at the time of Creation, but man chose to go his own way. The Lord plotted the path for Abraham into an unknown land. He led the children of Israel out of Egypt with a cloud by day, and a pillar of fire by night. Later Jesus would say, "Follow Me."

The pioneers respected, above all, the man who knew the trail well. He knew best when the wagon train should hold up, and when it should press on. He knew the parts of the trail that would most severely test the wagons, the men, the stock. He knew those places where the enemy would most likely lurk.

Our Lord and Saviour has gone before us. He has walked upon planet Earth and endured everything the enemy could possibly throw at Him, or at us. He knows the terrain, because God the Son created Heaven and earth itself. He knows the limits of man, and the limits of the enemy. When He arose from the grave, He conquered all, including death, and opened the way for man to proceed and live forevermore.

The words of a familiar chorus assure us this:

My Lord knows the way through the wilderness:

All I have to do is follow.

Or to put it in the most simple of terms:

"I am the Way."

Suggestion:

See if you can find someone who remembers the tune to the chorus: "My Lord knows the way through the wilderness. All I have to do is follow."

You can secure more information on the Oregon Trail from the Nebraska Department of Economic Development, Division of Travel and Tourism, Box 94666, Lincoln, Nebraska 68509. Telephone: (402) 471-3111.

More About the Oregon Trail

You can follow some of the deep ruts of the Oregon Trail even today, especially in western Nebraska near Scottsbluff, a prominent landmark for the early pioneers. It is a massive brow of rock overhanging a pass, where thousands filed through, walking, riding west. Another landmark on the North Platte is Chimney Rock. A museum in Gering, Nebraska, near Scottsbluff, tells the story of the historic trail.

A short distance further west, you can still read clearly the names of some of the pioneers who left their autographs in the soft sandstone of Register Cliff!

At The Dalles, Oregon, which for many was the end of the Oregon Trail, townspeople gather every Easter in the city park for sunrise services. Nearby a marker indicates the spot where weary pioneers ended their long westward journey. Each year the preacher delivers his sermon from a basalt rock, using it as a makeshift pulpit. It is the same rock from which pioneer missionaries preached to local Indians more than one hundred years ago.

See also the story of Marcus and Narcissa Whitman.

Wagon train heading away from Chimney Rock.

12

Marcus Whitman.

Narcissa and Marcus Whitman

Can God turn our failures into His success?
How do you respond when you are misunderstood?

When the Indians misunderstood their good intent, tragedy struck. Christians will always have to live among those who don't understand.

Read: I Peter 2:21-25

In the Pacific Northwest, the names of missionaries Marcus and Narcissa Whitman would probably rank next to Lewis and Clark in a poll of famous pioneer duos.

Near Walla Walla in the southeastern corner of Washington, just over the Oregon border, the Whitman gravesites and a lonely, reconstructed mission station (now a national historic site) vividly remind tourists of what once happened here.

Dr. Whitman and his eastern-bred bride, Narcissa, had arrived in this Northwest wilderness in 1836 and opened a mission among the Cayuse at their landmark outpost on the Oregon Trail.

Like modern-day Wycliffe Translators, the missionaries eventually learned the Indian language and devised an alphabet.

Narcissa graciously hosted a growing parade of travelers on the Oregon Trail, taught school, handled endless nursing chores and anguished over keeping house under the eyes of the curious Indians who unreservedly walked in and out of the house.

But after years of work the Indians had shown little response to the gospel.

Then in 1847, an epidemic of measles broke out. Doctor Whitman's medicine helped the whites, but not the Indians, simply because they had no resistance to the disease. Within a short time half the tribe died.

The Indians misread this as a deliberate plot by the growing influx of white settlers.

On November 29, 1847, a band of Cayuse attacked the mission and killed Marcus Whitman, his wife and nearly a dozen others. A few survivors escaped, and fifty at the mission station were taken captive.

News of the tragedy sped to Congress in Washington, D.C., along with petitions from the settlers that the United States promptly establish territorial rule in the tense Northwest wilderness.

Congress acted, and the Oregon territory emerged.

Christians will always have to live among those, who, in one way or another, will inevitably misunderstand their intents.

Non-Christians usually perceive even reputable evangelists as "in it for the money." The public too often accommodates all kinds of immorality under the guise of "rights," then charges Christians with trying to "impose" their moral standards on others. Sometimes Christians simply don't fit in. The non-believer doesn't know what "makes him tick."

Even among the Christian brethren one can be misunderstood. One brother means right, by his actions, or his words, but another perceives it otherwise.

Our human reaction, when wronged, is almost always to defend ourselves. But what does today's scriptural passage reveal?

No one in history was so tragically misjudged, or accused unjustly, as was our Lord Jesus Christ. The suffering He endured, though He was innocent, is totally beyond our own experience. Yet He took the pain and the insults, and did not fight back, or try to get even. Instead, He left His case in the hands of God alone, who always judges fairly.

When misunderstood, you may simply have to leave your case in the hands of God, who has all the facts, and who alone judges fairly.

Jesus gave us the Supreme example. And in time God turned seeming tragedy into good, and wrong into right. "By His wounds you were healed" (I Peter 2:24 NASB).

More About the Whitmans

As early as the 1820s, a few explorers and traders had found their way into the Oregon country. Their reports eventually filtered to the East coast and helped trigger an interest among Christians in reaching the Indians with the gospel.

In western New York, Marcus Whitman, a 32-year-old medical doctor, answered the call. So also did the young but cultured Narcissa Prentiss, who was engaged to be his wife.

But would the American Board of Foreign Missions accept an "unmarried female" for the Oregon mission?

Almost everyone had advised against it, but Whitman, after an 1835 trial journey to the Rockies with the American Fur Company caravan, concluded that "where wagons could go, women could go."

At that time a wagon had not yet rumbled all the way to Oregon, but the doctor was determined to try both with the wagon and the woman.

The two were married and immediately headed West on their honeymoon trek to Oregon.

The seven-month journey proved extremely arduous. They contended with sick companions, frustrating delays, a slow-moving cattle herd and an unwieldy wagon. Marcus had to leave his wagon—reduced to a two-wheeled cart—at Fort Boise before crossing the Blue Mountains, where he could follow only the trails of Indians and trappers.

Through all of this, his wife Narcissa maintained a deep and abiding faith in the Lord—revealed years later in a diary she had kept on the trek. Along with another missionary wife, Eliza Spaulding, she became the first white woman to cross the Rocky Mountains.

While their mission work may have appeared to fail, the Whitmans' spiritual dedication left a splendid example to the nation. After their death, many other dedicated Christians responded to missions. And Narcissa left Americans a volume of richly detailed letters offering later generations a fascinating glimpse into Western pioneer life.

Why has God given us the Holy Spirit?
Do you rely on the Holy Spirit?

13 The Vanishing Windmill

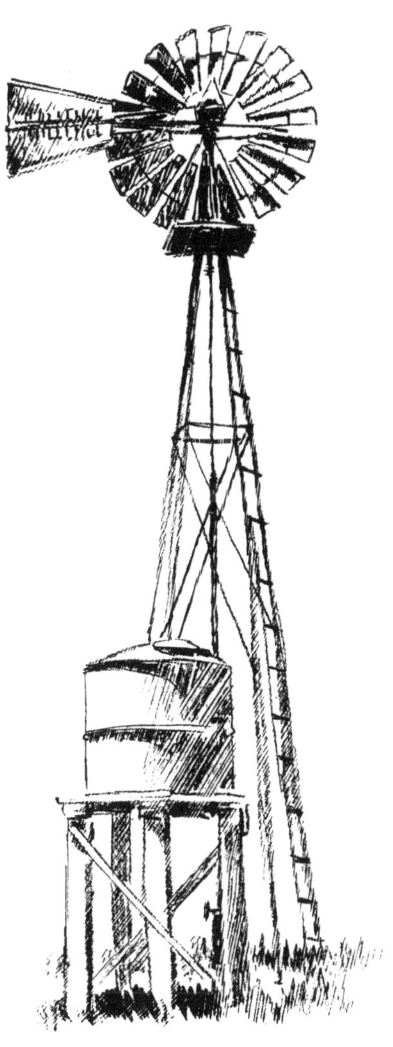

Let the oldtime windmill help give you some insights on the Christian life, and the power of the Holy Spirit.

Read: John 3:6-8

In the early part of this century nearly every farm in the American Midwest, and the West as well, had at least one windmill—sometimes several of them. The windmills were usually geared to a pump that could be detached and operated by hand. They could pump water from great depths to quench the thirst of livestock, irrigate gardens and provide cool water for farms and small-town households.

Today windmills can still be found, but you have to look a lot harder for them. And many of those you might spot across the countryside no longer pump water. Sometimes the farmer has simply let his old windmill stand because it is doing no harm, and because it reminds him of the past.

Electrical power has helped drive the windmill from the American landscape. Such power can fail at times, as in a bad storm, but not as often as the wind. Without wind, there is no water. The author grew up on a Western ranch that relied on a "windcharger" to generate power for the family's console radio. For about two weeks every October, because of little wind, the radio would inevitably go dead.

It's interesting how fickle and dependent windmills are, and how they react to those unseen forces around them. Changing winds toss the windmill's vanes to and fro, first in one direction, then another. Some Christians are like that. They go with the wind. They'll agree first with one friend or teacher, then with another who may come along and say just the opposite. Paul describes them in Ephesians 4:14 as "children, tossed to and fro, and carried about with every wind of doctrine." Jesus refers to a man of wishy-washy bent as like "a reed shaken with the wind" (Matthew 11:7).

In John 3 the Scriptures use the wind to describe the nature of the Holy Spirit. "The wind blows where it wishes and you hear the sound of it," the Bible says, "but do not know where it comes from and where it is going; so is everyone who is born of the Spirit" (verse 8).

We cannot see the Holy Spirit, as we cannot see the wind, yet we can see its effects. In a brisk breeze, the windmill turns easily. It works as it should. Many Christians, like windmills, stand idle or barely move, because there is no vigorous wind of the Holy Spirit blowing through their lives.

Windmills can be locked also, so that they do not spin, even in a strong wind. This reminds us of Christians who seem locked into idleness, even when things are happening around them. The gears of the same windmill can be disengaged so that the mill may spin furiously, but pump no water or generate no power. So are those Christians whose fins of busy church activity sometimes beat the air, but with little result. They feed no thirsty souls and generate no power.

It is a tragedy because our Creator and Saviour is the Master of the winds, who would empower us for every good work. The Book of Proverbs asks, "Who hath gathered the wind in his fists?" (30:4). Try it sometime, and you will have nothing to show. Yet God controls all wind currents—throughout the universe and encompasses all. It was Jesus, the Son of God, who demonstrated His power over all nature when He rebuked the winds upon the waters of Galilee and stilled the stormy sea.

This same Lord of the winds wants to see the Holy Spirit blow afresh in your life today.

More Facts About Windmills

Windmills have been known since at least the Middle Ages. In Holland they have been used for pumping water to reclaim land from the sea.

Studies at Oklahoma State University suggest that by building wind-energy conversion systems inland and offshore, the United States could generate five to ten percent of the country's projected total electric power needs by the year two thousand. The most promising high-wind areas in the United States are the Atlantic coast, the Great Plains, and the Pacific coast.

Winds of less than five miles per hour will not start up a windmill. Extremely high winds, as in a hurricane, make windmills hazardous and unsafe.

Has the meaning of patriotism changed?
Do you know how the national anthem testifies of God?

Beyond the Star Spangled Banner

Blind patriotism is not enough. When Francis Scott Key wrote America's national anthem, he insisted that the nation's future would have to rest on godly foundations.

Read: Psalm 33:1-12

On Chesapeake Bay in August 1814, British ships bombard Baltimore's Fort McHenry relentlessly throughout the night. As dawn breaks, Francis Scott Key peers anxiously through a pair of powerful field glasses. His eyes try to pierce the lingering haze and smoke of battle, along with a morning mist. Surely, he fears, the fort has fallen, and with it may go his beloved nation.

Suddenly Key sees it, and stares in disbelief. The flag is still there!

The moment so inspired him that he promptly wrote an immortal poem —some say on the back of an old letter—that one day would become America's national anthem.

The lyrics he wrote are full of patriotism, but they go much beyond. That's because Francis Scott Key was not only a patriot, but a born-again Christian. Military might, emotional patriotism, he knew, was not enough. His historic lyrics even imply that his country, in the future, might not always be right (". . . If our cause it is just"). "If this be our motto," he insists, "in God is our trust."

It is the same thrust of today's text, Psalm 33. Only the Lord deserves our supreme trust (verse 4). He loves all that is just and good.

Moreover, the Lord alone is the Creator who made the galaxies (verse 6) and the oceans (verse 7). Therefore let the entire earth stand in awe of Him (verse 8). When He spoke, the world began (verse 9).

The Lord can utterly frustrate the plans of those nations, and those people, who defy Him (verse 10). His own plans of righteousness do not change (verse 11). It may not always seem that way in the short term, either among individuals or nations, but it will be so when all the returns are in.

And then comes the pivotal statement of this Psalm, for all governments and all peoples. "Blessed is the nation whose God is the Lord;

Francis Scott Key.

and the people whom he hath chosen for his own inheritance" (verse 12).

Read beyond verse 12 as well, and it will be clear that God alone enjoys "the big view." Nothing escapes the Lord—either what men do, or what they think. Nor can military might alone, apart from righteousness, ultimately prevail (verses 16-17).

Francis Scott Key understood the Judeo-Christian foundations of the country he so loved. On a personal basis, he sought to win others to Jesus Christ. If our nation should wander from its foundations, he believed, it would soon be in trouble. As one of the nation's most able lawyers and statesmen of his time, he served his nation well.

It was Francis Scott Key, author of our national anthem, who in 1824 helped found the American Sunday School Union, a vigorous movement which started thousands of Sunday Schools across the nation in those early days. In fact, he served as its Vice-President for some eighteen years.

Even as a small boy, say the documents, Key learned many hymns and would read the Bible aloud to his own family. In later years, as a Christian statesman, he took time, on occasion, to jot down lyrics of praise. In the spirit of the opening verses of Psalm 33, his life truly brought honor to the Lord.

Song of Praise

Five years after Francis Scott Key wrote "The Star Spangled Banner," he also wrote, "Lord, With Glowing Heart I'd Praise Thee," which still appears in some church hymnals. Its words reveal the depths of the author's faith:

Lord, with glowing heart I'd praise Thee,
For the bliss Thy love bestows;
For the pardoning grace that saves me,
And the peace that from it flows.

Help, O God, my weak endeavor;
This dull soul to rapture raise;
Thou must light the flame, or never
Can my love be warmed to praise.

Almost Like Real

Baltimore—1983. Ships fire their guns on Chesapeake Bay. Fireworks explode above Fort McHenry. The smoke of battle settles in. Thousands watch as the Stars and Stripes fly proudly against a blackened sky.

It happens every September, on Defenders Day, when Fort McHenry reenacts the historic battle that gave birth to our national anthem.

At least one half million people a year still visit Fort McHenry. There many put themselves, mentally, back into the past, relive the bombardment, and wander through the little fort that once rocked and shook for one long day and one long night.

The Battle of Baltimore, 1814.

15

Should Christians stand up for their beliefs even though it's unpopular?

How can you be courageous in your faith?

When Garfield Took His Stand

It would have been easy for young Jim Garfield to join in the drinks and go along with the crowd. But the future President handled it another way.

Read: II Timothy 1:7-9

It had been a day for the students at Williams College in Massachusetts, and no one had enjoyed it more than Jim Garfield. Now the school's annual "Mountain Day Frolic," which always included a climb of nearby Mount Greylock, was about to come to a close.

The students assembled to celebrate with some alcoholic beverages. They turned to Garfield, one of their most popular colleagues, to lead them in the festivities.

Jim Garfield had once been a rough and tough teenage sailor on the Erie Canal—until the day he nearly drowned. He was saved from sure death only when a towrope looped just right to catch the rim of the barge, where he could pull himself to safety. That night he tried six hundred times, without success, to make the rope repeat its act. "Only God saved me," he concluded.

Not long after his close call, Jim Garfield opened his heart to the Lord at an Ohio camp meeting and the next day was baptized in the ice-cold waters of the Chagrin River.

Now would Jim Garfield, the Christian, simply take the easy road out with his friends? After all, he could reason, surely this hilarious occasion called for it.

But Jim Garfield knew he had made the mistake once before. Back on the Erie Canal, before his con-

James Garfield as president.

version, he had let some of his raucous friends begin to dictate his lifestyle.

With perfect calmness, Jim Garfield pulled a battered Bible from his pocket. He told his startled friends that it was his habit to read a chapter from the Bible every evening. "Shall I read aloud?" he asked.

No one objected. So Garfield read.

There are times when Christians have to take a stand. In the spirit of today's passage, they dare not be "ashamed" of the gospel.

Several years ago the long-time employee of a major Midwestern printing firm refused to be involved in the printing of pornographic magazines. Because of his Christian conviction, he lost his job.

In Minnesota a Christian nurse at a major hospital refused to participate in abortions. Her courage brought hundreds of other nurses "out of the woodwork" to stand with her, and make national headlines.

The long-time chief executive of a major American motel chain resigned when, in Christian conscience, he could not be a part of a firm whose board had decided to venture into casino gambling. It was his own decision, and he stepped down graciously, and without rancor. Yet he made clear to all, his conscience on the matter.

Such courage may invite derision from a few, but in most cases it draws repect. Underneath it all, even the critics are often saying, "I wish I had that kind of courage and conviction."

Christians who take a stand are not "unbalanced." The Scriptures in this passage from II Timothy assure us that "God hath not given us the spirit of fear; but of power, and of love, and of a sound mind" (verse 7).

When we know without doubt that God has called us to His own purposes, by His own grace, it is no longer so difficult to take a stand. And to think that God's plans were initiated even "before the world began" (see verse 9)!

Jim Garfield must have sensed something of a greater call and purpose.

In 1880, he was elected President of the United States.

Garfield in Debate

James Garfield was the only United States president who was also a preacher—and a good one at that. He once baptized forty converts during a two-week evangelistic campaign.

On another occasion, as a young man in his home state of Ohio, he took on an atheist by the name of Denton in a series of public debates on the issues of evolution. His foe was a rapid, elegant, fiery speaker who had argued the subject in public forty times. To prepare himself, Garfield crammed for weeks in geology, physiology, and other sciences.

The debate ran for five days, with two sessions a day. Hundreds, even thousands, turned out. Denton tried his best to invalidate the claims of the Bible and "remove God from immediate control of the universe." But Garfield countered his opponent at every turn, point for point.

By all accounts, Denton's evolution had been demolished by the time the debate was over.

Question

In what ways can you "take your stand" for Jesus?

Does God fit into education? How? Where? Should your education include the Bible?

16

God and the "Ivy League"

Harvard, Yale, Princeton, Dartmouth—all once insisted there could be no true education without a knowledge of the Lord Jesus Christ.

Read: Proverbs 9:10

They're known as the oldest universities in the country, and among the best—Harvard, Yale, Princeton, Dartmouth. The ivy that covers the brick-walled buildings on these historic campuses, all in New England, explains the term, "Ivy League."

It may come as a surprise to you that all of these famous schools were founded by Christians.

Harvard College's first presidents and tutors insisted that there could be no true knowledge or wisdom without Jesus Christ. Harvard's "rules and precepts" adopted in 1646 included the following essentials:

"Every one shall consider the main end of his life and studies to know God and Jesus Christ which is eternal life.

"Seeing the Lord giveth wisdom, every one shall seriously by prayer in secret seek wisdom of Him." Harvard students were to read the Scriptures twice a day and fifty-two percent of the seventeenth-century Harvard graduates became ministers!

Christians in the Connecticut region launched Yale, also to train ministers. Princeton (originally called "The College of New Jersey") sprang up in part from the great religious revival that swept New England in the early 1700s, which became known as the First Great Awakening. Dartmouth was founded as a missionary school to reach the Indians with the gospel. Unfortunately, these schools eventually lost their original Christian focus.

The founders of these early Ivy League schools understood clearly the meaning of Proverbs 9:10, that "The fear of the Lord is the beginning of wisdom: and the knowledge of the Holy One is understanding" (NASB). The Book of Proverbs, in fact, centers on the theme of wisdom and makes clear that true wisdom has its source in the Maker of the universe.

Much of today's education, however, ignores this. Subtly it has removed God from the center of the universe and put man in His place. From the sciences to sociology and psychology, it has omitted God and moved man to front-center. No wonder it struggles so desperately to explain the origin of the universe and of man. It omits God on the argument of "academic freedom," while at the same time it denies that same freedom to those with a Christian world view.

There is nothing wrong with acquiring knowledge, but a man's education these days will fall short if he does not sift all of this through the screen of the Scriptures.

When America's early Christian schools forsook their original mission, others came along to take their places. These include the Bible Institutes and Bible colleges that began to spring up in the late 1880s. Today the Christian schools movement, which starts even at the kindergarten level, is booming across America.

Anyone today can secure a Christian eduction, if he puts his mind to it. Those beyond their early years of education can read Christian books, take Bible correspondence courses, or maybe even attend an evening school at a local Bible Institute.

Every Christian family already owns the prime Textbook, which of course is the Bible itself, available today in all kinds of versions and with a smorgasbord of study aids.

Study the Bible eagerly, let the Holy Spirit have freedom in your life, and you will be building the foundations upon which all true wisdom and knowledge rests. "Grow in grace, and in the knowledge of our Lord and Saviour Jesus Christ. To him be glory both now and forever. Amen" (II Peter 3:18).

Yale: Little-Known Facts

Though Yale was founded as a Christian school in 1701, its religious atmosphere had declined when Timothy Dwight became president in 1795. Many students had become "skeptics." Dwight met their criticism head-on in a series of frank discussions and chapel messages. As a result, a revival began in which a third of the student body professed conversion.

Yale President Timothy Dwight was the author of a hymn still sung in many churches, and possibly your own:

I love Thy Kingdom, Lord,
The house of Thine abode,
The Church our blest Redeemer saved
With His own precious blood.

In 1828 the "Illinois Band," composed of fourteen dedicated Yale theological students, went forth to evangelize Illinois. This group triggered other similar movements throughout the territory and helped make Yale an influential national institution.

What qualities cause you to respect someone?
How can you know that your plans are God's will?

17

Following the Right Steps

The boy followed gigantic footprints that someone had left in the snow. Whose were they, and where would they lead?

Read: Psalm 37:23-24

One crisp winter night during the Civil War, a young boy made his way through the snow that had freshly fallen on Washington, D.C. Suddenly he halted. In front of him were the biggest footprints he had ever seen.

Curious who may have made them, he decided to follow them for a while and see where they led.

The boy tramped onward, finding it no problem to keep on the man's trail. The steps led to the side door of a Presbyterian church.

The boy gently opened the door just enough to peek in.

The man he saw, sitting alone, was the President of the United States, Abraham Lincoln. It was prayer meeting night, but Lincoln sat in an alcove off to the side, unnoticed by the others present.

The boy remembered that scene vividly for the rest of his life.

This boy had followed in the steps of a great man. But the steps could have just as easily been those of a drunkard headed for the nearest neighborhood tavern. The boy could not have made a better choice. Today's young generation still needs to follow the right men, and the right examples.

Psalm 37 says that "the steps of a good man are ordered by the Lord: and he delighteth in his way" (verse 23). He is pleased with each step such a man takes, because he knows right from wrong.

This does not mean every step is perfect. Sometimes even good men slip a bit, but their Lord is always there to pull them upright again, or back onto the right path.

Other Scriptures, too, talk about the steps of men. "A man's heart deviseth his way," says Proverbs 16:9, "but the Lord directeth his steps." The statement may seem at first like a contradiction, but it simply means that although even godly men have to make most of their own plans, they had better count on God to direct those plans.

After all, man has so few of the facts. God, on the other hand, sees the end from the beginning. "It is not in man that walketh to direct his steps," says Jeremiah 10:23. It is not within the power of man alone to map his life, and to get it right. That's why we need God to direct our course.

But how? Psalm 119, longest in the Bible, has the clue. "Order my steps in thy word: and let not any iniquity have dominion over me" (Psalm 119:133).

And who cannot be moved by the classic in I Peter 2? No man in history was so falsely accused as was our Lord when He permitted Himself to be crucified. Yet He did not fight back, because He knew He was doing just what God the Father wanted Him to do. If necessary, we too should be willing to suffer for the sake of the gospel. Jesus Christ left us an example, says the Scriptures, that we should "follow His steps (verse 21)."

The idea is so well expressed in the old hymn, "Footsteps of Jesus."

**Sweetly, Lord, have we heard
Thee calling,
Come, follow Me!
And we see where Thy footsteps
falling
Lead us to Thee.**

**Footsteps of Jesus, that make
the pathway glow;
We will follow the steps of Jesus
where'er they go.**

It does make a difference whose footprints you follow.

Suggestion:

Ask your friends or relatives who they think are the five greatest United States presidents. Keep track of how many people list Lincoln. How many places do you know of that are named after President Lincoln?

Lincoln Look-alike

People magazine called him "a dead ringer for Abe Lincoln."

"People take one look at him," it reported, "and gasp in mock horror, 'Hey, I thought you were dead!' "

It happens constantly to the Rev. Bruce Hanks, especially when he dresses up in a black frock coat, black bow tie, and stovepipe hat.

Bruce Hanks, Lincoln Look-Alike.

He is tall, thin, a little gangling. His facial features are like Lincoln's as is his hairstyle and his beard.

He is the same size as Lincoln (6 feet 4 inches, 190 pounds), and he even has a wart on his cheek where our sixteenth president had his.

But that isn't all. He is actually a distant cousin of Nancy Hanks, Lincoln's mother!

Rev. Hanks is a Baptist pastor in Minnesota. But during the 1976 bicentennial year, and the years around it, Hanks took a leave of absence from the pulpit to make the rounds of schools, churches, and civic and farm organizations throughout the United States. He spent two summers in New Salem, Illinois, where Lincoln once lived, and put on six performances each day at the state park there.

Though back in the pulpit now, Hanks still travels some. Usually he delivers a slide lecture about Lincoln's life and then delivers the Gettysburg Address.

Students rarely forget the day "Abraham Lincoln" comes to their school.

The two questions they ask most are, "Are you really a relative of Abraham Lincoln?" and "Is that a real beard?"

To both questions his answer is "yes."

There's one more coincidence. Lincoln's wife's name was Mary Ann Todd. Bruce Hanks' wife's name is also Mary Ann!

Does God need man-made buildings to convey His greatness? What has God done to prove His greatness to you?

Nashville's Parthenon and the Sermon on Mars Hill

God created the universe, but as in the day of Paul's great speech in Athens, men are still trying to confine the Creator to their own little structures.

Read: Acts 17:16-34

For many centuries the majestic Parthenon, most famous of all the ancient Greek temples, sat high on the Acropolis in the city of Athens. Then one day in 1787, the great structure suddenly exploded. Today only a shell of the original Parthenon remains.

But you may be surprised to learn that the Parthenon lives on, not necessarily in the ancient land of Greece, but right here in the United States. In Nashville, Tennessee, long known as the "Athens of the South," you can find a remarkable replica of the Parthenon, completed in 1931. About a million people a year come to see it.

The original Parthenon, dedicated to the goddess Athena, must have fascinated the Apostle Paul as he strolled amid the great structures of ancient Athens.

It must have also troubled his heart.

For here was a beautiful building, built at great cost by skilled and intelligent people—in honor of a goddess that didn't even exist!

The Greeks had so many such gods, in fact, that they had even built an altar to the "unknown god," to be sure they did not miss one!

No wonder Paul stood in the midst of all this on Mars Hill and declared to the crowds around him a living God who far transcends even the greatest monuments that man can build.

"He made the world and everything in it," roared Paul, "and since He is Lord of Heaven and earth, He doesn't live in manmade temples."

God not only made the universe, says Paul, but He also made man. He further explained that God created all the people of the world from one man, Adam, and scattered the nations across the face of the earth. God decided beforehand which

Ruins of the ancient Parthenon in Athens, Greece.

should rise and fall, and when. He determined their boundaries.

Paul's great sermon on Mars Hill also makes clear that God is the author of all life. "He Himself gives life and breath to everything."

But Paul really clinches this truth when, a few verses later, he jolts his audience with the truth of the Resurrection.

God will judge those listening, says Paul, and in fact ultimately the whole world. "Because he hath appointed a day, in the which he will judge the world in righteousness by that man whom he hath ordained; whereof he hath given assurance unto all men, in that he hath raised him from the dead" (verse 31).

In some ways the world has not changed a whole lot since the days of ancient Greece. Men are still trying to confine God in their own little structures, while they ignore Him as Creator of all. Evolution today refuses to grant that God created man and the universe. Many insist such ideas are not good science. Yet they attempt to explain our world and the existence of life itself with theories that would take incredible "faith" to believe! Is this really "open-minded" science?

More About the Parthenon

The Parthenon in Athens is said to have been the most perfect building ever erected by man. There was not a straight line in the building. Columns bowed slightly at the top to avoid optical illusions of sagging lines or crooked columns.

Though the Parthenon in Nashville is the exact size of the original, its materials are different. The real Parthenon was made of marble. The one in Nashville is of reinforced concrete and crushed colored tile (floors are Tennessee marble). Yet its colors are correct—precisely the same as fragments of the original Parthenon salvaged from the ruins at Athens.

As in the days of the ancient Parthenon, masses of people still walk the streets pursuing their own speculations and philosophical fads. They remain ignorant of the One who truly gives life. To them He is still unknown.

Paul's great sermon on Mars Hill reminds us that the destinies of nations are still in God's hands, and someday all history will culminate in Jesus Christ. He alone can give eternal life, meaning and purpose to this generation. You **can** truly know Him.

19

Do Christians have a responsibility to share the gospel?
Do you look for opportunities to share the gospel of Christ?

The Pony Express: A Lesson in Relay

Pony Express riders relayed urgent mail cross-country. Christians must relay the gospel from one generation to another.

Read: Psalm 145:1-4

The famous Pony Express of yesteryear whisked the mail across the western wilderness from St. Louis to Sacramento in just ten days.

But it took an elaborate relay system to make it work, complete with four hundred horses, some eighty young riders, plus station keepers, stock tenders, route superintendents, and shuttling supply wagons.

Over that historic rugged trail of 1,840 miles, the mail changed hands no less than one hundred fifty-seven times.

Yet it inevitably made it through.

It could never have happened had there not always been a rider at the next station, ready to grab the mail sack, thunder the next five to twenty miles, and in turn pass it on.

When the Apostle Paul answered the Macedonian call (Acts 16:10), he planted the gospel in Europe and started a "gospel relay express," so to speak, that has endured on down through the centuries.

It has always taken someone to pass it on.

When the Puritans planted their Massachusetts Bay Colony, they also imported the gospel, and started such schools as Harvard and later Yale to assure that there would be an adequate supply of trained ministers of the gospel to "pass it on."

When Roger Williams founded the colony of Rhode Island and later planted the first Baptist church in America, he set in motion a whole movement that would help spread the gospel far and wide.

The early Methodist circuit riders blazed the wilderness frontier with their preaching and their Christian tracts. They fanned the flames of revival, and thousands found Jesus Christ.

Later, evangelists like Charles Finney, Dwight L. Moody and Billy Sunday would preach to millions. Many of their converts in turn, would "pass it on."

If you know the Lord as your Saviour, you can be especially grateful for the long line of witnesses who have passed on the gospel message,

These two U.S. Postage Stamps commemorate the Pony Express.

and particularly for those who have directly influenced your life.

But what of today?

Psalm 145 gives us some interesting insights.

"One generation shall praise thy works to another," says this Psalm, "and shall declare thy mighty acts (verse 4)."

That means each of us today who knows the gospel is expected to pass it on. But note the dynamic involved:

"I will extol thee, my God, O king . . . I will praise thy name . . . Great is the Lord, and greatly to be praised; and his greatness is unsearchable."

The Christian who has a grasp of God's greatness finds it a natural thing to praise the Lord, both in his personal devotional life and among those with whom he walks.

Questions

Who was the one (or who were the ones) who passed the gospel on to you?

What have you done with it?

What are some ways you can share the gospel with someone else?

More about the Pony Express

Though its reputation spread far and wide, the Pony Express only operated for eighteen months—from April, 1860 to October, 1861.

Riders of the Pony Express were required, by the General Superintendent, to carry a Bible.

You can still visit the original stables of the Pony Express at the start of its route—in St. Joseph, Missouri.

Suggestion

Read or sing a stanza of the song, "Pass It On," and compare it to I John 4:11.

The stables of the Pony Express in St. Joseph, Missouri.

20

Does God want Christians to succeed?
Does your attitude improve your performance?

From a Young Newscarrier: Do Your Best

Some of America's greatest men of success were once newscarriers. Paperboy Greg Enos suggests the kind of attitude that may have helped them succeed.

Read: I Corinthians 13:1-7

At the American Freedoms Foundation in Valley Forge, Pennsylvania—in a building overlooking the very meadow where George Washington once drilled his troops—there's an unusual exhibit.

There you can wander through a photo gallery of more than one hundred famous Americans who started on their paths to fame—as newscarriers.

Who are they?

Well, men like the late General Omar Bradley and President Dwight D. Eisenhower.

Journalists like Drew Pearson and Art Buchwald.

Earl Warren, former Chief Justice of the United States Supreme Court.

Former President Jimmy Carter is among them.

Newscarrier Greg Enos delivers the Palo Alto (California) **Times**.

In fact, this exhibit of more than one hundred celebrities includes a cross-section of figures from almost every major occupational field. Each achieved success.

What kind of newscarriers were they?

In most cases we really don't know. But probably most of them were very good ones.

Why? Because sloppy newscarriers don't show the qualities that lead to success.

They're the ones, who, if they miss the target, will leave the paper in the bushes. After all, someone will find it eventually.

They're the ones who find easy excuses to miss deliveries, or who start out only when they feel like it.

Greg Enos of Sunnyvale, California (see photo) was delivering the **Peninsula Times Tribune** when he wrote "a paperboy's paraphrase" of I Corinthians 13—as a class assignment at nearby Valley Christian Junior High School.

Here is what he had to say:

"If I could throw my paper route blindfolded, but did not have love for each of my customers, I would be just as well off sitting in a closet the rest of my life.

"And if I could porch any house I wanted with my backhand shot, but did not have love, it would mean nothing. And if I could fold one hundred papers in five minutes, but did not have love, my time would be worthless.

"Love is patient when you have to go back to a customer five times to get him to pay you. Love is kind when those mean kids throw their football at you.

"Love isn't jealous when you hear of another paperboy making one hundred and fifty dollars a month and you only make fifty.

"Love is not proud even when you have a reputation for never throwing a paper on a roof or breaking a window. Love does not demand its own way when it's raining and you would rather have your parents drive you.

"Tired aching legs, rainy days, flat tires, and frightening dogs will come to an end, but love is everlasting. Customers that are difficult to please will come to an end, but love is eternal. Paper routes will come to an end, but love never ends.

"Before I had my route, I thought only of my own desires; but now I understand that a frail, old lady needs to be able to find her paper on the porch on a dark night. And the weary businessman returning home needs to find his paper there on time.

"These three things I have learned on my route: endurance, patience, and love, but the greatest of these is love."*

This is the kind of spirit that will open doors to success. It's the spirit that says, "I'm here to serve you." The truly great leaders are not arrogant know-it-alls, but humble servants. Jesus set the example. He came not to be served, but to serve.

Greg Enos will go places, and so will others like him. Anyone who takes a job, old or young, needs his attitude.

Whatever job you tackle, do your best.

Question:

How does Colossians 3:17 fit the spirit of Greg Enos' paraphrase?

*Used by permission.

21

Does Christianity guarantee a life free of difficulties? How do you rebound from failure or disappointment?

J. C. Penney.

The God Who Cares

Merchandiser J. C. Penney built his chain of department stores into a fortune, only to lose it all in the stock market crash of 1929. How and why did he bounce back?

Read: I Peter 5:7

The name of J. C. Penney is known far and wide. Not too many know, however, that he was the son of a Baptist minister. With no room for compromise, the father built into his son's life the principles of absolute honesty. As a young man, J. C. Penney adopted the Golden Rule as his business ethic, and in a few years he built his store chain into one of the nation's giants.

Then in 1929, the stock market crashed. Penney's fortune crashed with it and he personally lost nine million dollars. By 1932 Penney had to sell out to pay his debts. It left him almost bankrupt. The trauma affected his health, and he wound up in a hospital in Battle Creek, Michigan.

Early one morning, in the depths of despair, Penney woke to hear the distant singing of employees who had gathered to start the day praising God.

They were singing "Be not dismayed, whate'er betide; God will take care of you . . ."

Penney followed the music down the hallway to its source, a chapel, and slipped into the back row.

When he left a short time later he was a changed man, and ready to start the long climb back to health.

Step by step, Penney began to rebuild his chain of department stores across America. It grew into an empire even much larger than it had ever been before. Strong in Christian character, J. C. Penney gave much of his new fortune to Christian causes throughout the rest of his career.

Tragedy of one kind or another can break a man's spirit to an extent that he never recovers. Even minor disappointments may convince us, for a time, that God doesn't really care.

That is Satan's lie. The Scripture says to cast all your anxieties upon God, "for He careth for you" (verse 7).

In adverse circumstances, what attitudes are most likely to reveal this great truth?

One is a humble spirit. First Peter 5 stresses this in the context of leadership. Power struggles and church squabbles destroy the climate for God's blessing. A humble spirit can not only heal church wounds, but also lift the burden of personal anxieties.

The one in a crisis tends to feel he's alone in his trouble. It is not so. When the crash ruined J. C. Penney's fortune, it also ruined the fortunes of others. Some committed suicide because they couldn't handle it. Paul reminds his readers that others of his own Christian brethren around the world are also going through affliction (verse 9).

An attitude of patience must also prevail. The Lord may assure you of His care in a time of crisis, but you want the trial removed—now. It may not be so immediate. Yet time and time again God, in His own due time, picks up the pieces and lifts up the fallen.

If you doubt God's care, it may take a little time for Him to convince you otherwise.

It did for J. C. Penney.

Questions

When you have let sin throw you onto the mat, take hold of the promise of I John 1:9. Why do you think some have called this passage "the doctrine of the re-bound"?

Suggestion

Sing together the hymn that inspired J. C. Penney to make a comeback ("Be not dismayed whate'er betide; God will take care of you. . . ").

Can the greatest forces of nature compare to God's strength? What does nature teach you about God?

Our Mountains: What Do They Say?

The peaks and ranges of America, coupled with a study of the Scriptures, can teach you something about the nature of God.

Read: Psalm 90:1-2

The United States has been blessed with its many beautiful mountain ranges. The Rockies, for instance, rise abruptly from the Great Central Plains, sending more than fifty peaks above the 14,000-foot level.

Farther west, the Sierras form another high barrier, walling in California and forcing much of the Pacific ocean moisture from the skies before it can reach the deserts beyond.

In the northwest, rise the heavily-forested Cascades, with their string of mostly dormant volcanic peaks stretching from Mount Baker in Washington State to as far south as Mount Shasta and Mount Lassen in northern California.

Until the mid-Twentieth Century, California's 14,494-foot Mount Whitney stood as the highest pinnacle in the land—a shade higher even than any peak in the Rockies. But when Alaska joined the Union, California had to move aside to make room for Mount McKinley, which rises to more than 20,000 feet. And with Hawaii's admission, the United States inherited still other impressive peaks like Mauna Kea.

Once every great while, in Hawaii or Alaska, one of these peaks would erupt, throwing steam, fire and ash into the atmosphere. But until 1980, it had not happened on the U. S. mainland for more than sixty years. Then one Sunday afternoon, after rumbling and spewing off and on for several weeks, Washington's Mount St. Helens blew.

Mountains force us to stand in awe. Among them there is a kind of spiritual presence. The Scriptures seem to recognize this—the Psalms in particular. One could almost worship the mountains, and in some cultures men have. But the Scriptures always use them to point us to God, who transcends all: We are told that:

Before the mountains were created, before the earth was formed, there was God who is without beginning or end (Psalm 90:2).

The explosion of Mount St. Helens, May, 1980.

Rustic chapel against the Grand Tetons.

Behind the mountains that rise stands the One who made them, for He formed the mountains by His mighty strength (Psalm 65:6).

He controls the formation of the deep places of the earth, and the highest mountains belong to Him (Psalm 95:4).

He holds the world together so that it will never fall apart. Like a garment He covered the earth with water, even covering the mountains. He spoke with a voice like thunder and the mountains rose up and the waters collected in the great ocean beds and in valleys, as He decreed. Also, He set a boundary for the waters so they will never again cover the earth. (Psalm 104:5-9).

The mountains unfold just a glimpse of God's greatness so that even the mountains and hills praise the Lord. He alone is worthy. (Psalm 148:9,13).

And the majestic mountains cannot compare with Him for glory. (Psalm 76:4).

The mountains may seem as if they will last forever, but they won't. They gradually (and sometimes not so gradually) wear away, and sometimes rebuild. Mount St. Helens demonstrated dramatically what can happen. In a matter of seconds, one huge blast blew away nearly 1,500 feet of the mountain top, and in those moments all maps showing the peak at 9,677 feet became outdated!

Therefore, we need not fear even though the earth changes and mountains shake, and are carried into the sea. (Psalm 46:1-3).

God is our refuge and strength, and He remains unchanged.

Let the mountains always remind you of God.

Mountainous Questions

On what mountain did God give Moses the Ten Commandments?

On what mountain was Jesus transfigured?

On what mountain will Jesus return?

Pike's Peak

True or false: Pike's Peak is taller than Washington state's Mount Rainier and California's Mount Shasta. Answer: False. Mount Rainier is 14,410 feet, Mount Shasta 14,162 feet, and Pike's Peak 14,110 feet. In fact, thirty other peaks in Colorado are just slightly higher than Pike's Peak!

Pike's Peak, though, is one of two mountains in the United States over 14,000 feet with a road to the top (Mount Evans of Colorado being the other). You can also take a cog railroad up Pike's Peak. It is the highest railroad in the United States, and the highest cog road in the world. The round trip by train takes three hours and ten minutes.

Suggestion:

This would be an appropriate time to sing at least one stanza of "America, the Beautiful."

Can Christian forgiveness heal the scars of war? How can the gospel bring peace to you?

Beyond Pearl Harbor

Mitsuo Fuchida led the fateful 1941 attack on Oahu that plunged the United States into World War II. When Sergeant Jake DeShazer heard the news in California, he hurled a potato against the wall in rage. Why, then, did the two later become friends?

Read: Colossians 3:12-15

On Sunday morning, December 7, 1941, a major part of the United States Pacific fleet rested lazily at anchor in Pearl Harbor, in the Hawaiian islands. Meanwhile, an ominous squadron of nearly two hundred Japanese war-planes streaked in from the north.

In command was Captain Mitsuo Fuchida. He kept his planes low—only three thousand meters above the water—to duck the enemy's radar.

Suddenly Fuchida sighted the fleet and called for the attack: "Tora! Tora! Tora!"

An hour later more than two thousand Americans were dead, the United States fleet had been largely destroyed, and the nation remained only hours away from official entry into World War II.

At an army camp mess hall in California, word of the sneak attack flashed over the radio. In a rage, Sergeant Jake DeShazer hurled a potato against the wall. "Just wait and see what we'll do to you!" he screamed at the enemy.

DeShazer later flew in a secret raid on Tokyo, but he had to parachute into hostile territory near Nanking and wound up a prisoner of

The attack on Pearl Harbor, December 7, 1941.

war. For more than two years DeShazer's hatred boiled—until one cold winter day when someone passed a Bible through his cell group. DeShazer began to study this Bible, his heart began to soften, and in time he asked the Lord into his life.

Fuchida, meanwhile, had hoped to become an admiral, but he saw his dreams fade as he sat out the Battle of Midway with appendicitis and learned that ten Japanese warships had gone down.

At the war's end, DeShazer earned his degree at Seattle Pacific University, an evangelical Christian school, and returned to Japan as a missionary.

Fuchida found himself out of work. Worried about the war trials to be held for the Japanese military, he returned to farming near Osaka. Though General MacArthur summoned him to the trials, it was not as a defendant, but only as a witness.

One day in 1950, as Fuchida got off a train in a Tokyo station, an American handed him a pamphlet. Its title: "I Was a Prisoner of Japan." Fuchida stuck it in his pocket and read it later. It was Sergeant Jake DeShazer's dramatic conversion story.

Fuchida could not explain, nor forget, what he had read. Though a Buddhist by tradition, he bought a Bible and began to search it. He was overwhelmed by the drama of the crucifixion, and especially by Christ's prayer shortly before His death: "Father, forgive them, for they know not what they do." The message hit him hard. He had slaughtered so many!

On April 12,1950, Fuchida became a Christian. The news shocked his family and made news-

paper headlines. Old war buddies tried to destroy his new faith. Many said it wouldn't last.

They were wrong. Fuchida began to speak out for Jesus and conduct crusades throughout Japan. For more than a quarter century, until shortly before his death in 1978, he continued to preach the gospel in his home country, in the United States, and on other continents, often in the presence of world leaders.

DeShazer appeared with Fuchida many times. The two soldiers, who had so many reasons to hate one another, would join together to demonstrate the power of the Prince of Peace!

What great power there is in forgiveness! At its deepest level, forgiveness among men can only root itself in God's forgiveness. When Jesus healed the man sick of palsy (see Matthew 9:6), He made it clear that only "the Son of man hath power on earth to forgive sins."

This is why Paul could say in Colossians 3:13, "Even as Christ forgave you, so also do ye."

In verses preceding this text, Paul contrasts the old man with the new man, and declares that the gospel can break down all barriers of nationality, education or social class (verse 11).

When Christ forgives, and guilt is removed by the blood of Jesus Christ, then the peace of God can rule in man's heart (verse 15).

The gospel of forgiveness can indeed make a difference between war and peace.

Question

When was the last time you forgave someone?

24

Does God give men the opportunity to honor Him?
How can you turn attention to Jesus when you succeed?

William Penn.

William Penn's Big Real Estate Deal

God singled out a devout man with a strong sense of social justice and trusted him with a remarkable expanse of American wilderness.

Read: James 3:13-18

It was 1670, a half century after the landing of the Pilgrims. In England, William Penn had just received a large inheritance from his father, Admiral Sir William Penn. The crown had owed the admiral a debt of 16,000 pounds, which was to be passed on to his son.

Instead of a cash settlement, young Penn petitioned the king for a tract of land in America "lying north of Maryland, on the east bounded with Delaware River, on the West . . . to extend as far as plantable, which is altogether Indian." In today's geography, that meant all the way to Ohio.

The venture might at first sound like the spoiled son out to spend his father's wealth on a wild speculative land scheme.

But note the young man's driving motive as he writes to a friend:

"I do, therefore, desire the Lord's wisdom to guide me, and those that may be concerned with me, that we do the thing that is truly wise and just."

William Penn, the peace-loving Quaker, wanted to open this vast wilderness to all peoples, regardless of religion, race or ethnic origin. The King of England gave to him what later became one of the largest states in the northeast United States —Pennsylvania—with right to govern. A year later the Duke of York also gave Penn what is now Delaware.

Penn clearly saw all of this as a trust from God. "I eyed the Lord in obtaining it," he wrote, "and more was I drawn inward to look to him, and to owe it to his hand and power than to any other way. I have so obtained it, and desire to keep it that I may not be unworthy of his love."

Some men might have grabbed this remarkable piece of real estate out of greed or selfish ambition. Not Penn. He wanted to honor the Lord, and to do that which is "wise and just."

Such is the kind of wisdom found in today's Scripture passage. It seeks the welfare of others, and puts Christian faith into action (verse 13). It does not act out of selfish ambition (verse 14). Men of true wisdom seek peace, not disorder (verses 16-18). The first is of God, the latter of Satan.

"For where envying and strife is, there is confusion and every evil work" (verse 16).

Sometimes nothing creates more chaos and disorder than a piece of real estate, especially when the owner dies, and would-be heirs fight over who is going to get the land, or its proceeds.

Imagine the value of Pennsylvania today! The dollars would be astronomical. But for Penn it was not a get-rich-quick scheme. He saw it as a potential land of liberty, and he advertised it far and wide, both on the Atlantic coast and in Europe. "The God who has given it me through many difficulties," said Penn, "will, I believe, bless and make it the seed of a nation."

Into this land poured the sons and daughters of many nations—the Dutch, the Swedes, the Welsh, English, Quakers, German groups and, last of all, the Scotch-Irish. Miles of forest stretching from Philadelphia to Pittsburgh soon accommodated peoples of all kinds—the persecuted from Europe, the smaller Protestant sects, Catholics, Jews.

William Penn's "Holy Experiment" survived to become a major cornerstone in the foundation of America. Perhaps it was because Penn understood that ultimately, all real estate belongs to God. "The earth is the Lord's, and the fulness thereof" (Psalm 24:1). Legally all property we own may be ours, but in reality it's only a temporary "trust from God" until life passes away.

And so it is with everything we own.

Questions

William Penn once wrote that "liberty without obedience is confusion, and obedience without liberty is slavery." What did he mean?

William Penn's 1681 treaty with the Indians.

Philadelphia, near Pennsylvania's eastern border, is the state's largest city and the scene of America's independence. Pittsburgh, the steel city near its western border, is second largest. What city is Pennsylvania's capital? Answer: Neither of these. It is Harrisburg, in the center of the state.

What qualifies God as the Master Artist?
Are you conforming to the image of Christ?

25

Faces in Stone

It took the skills of a master sculptor to shape the faces on Mount Rushmore. Behind every image is the work of a creator.

Read: I Corinthians 8:6; Ephesians 2:10

Travelers can see them for miles—the heads of four American Presidents carved in bold relief on the towering cliffs of a South Dakota mountain.

It took fourteen years to complete the gigantic project in the Black Hills. Bad weather and funding problems delayed its completion.

Sculptor Gutzon Borglum selected Mount Rushmore because it was smooth-grained granite, its 6,000-foot height dominated the surrounding terrain, and it faced the sun most of the day.

But it was hardly a place for conventional sculpturing techniques. Instead, it took the genius of an engineer as well.

Borglum first designed a grouping of the four Presidents to conform to the mountain's granite cap. But deep cracks and fissures later discovered in the rock required nine changes in the design.

Five-foot models of each figure guided the workmen on the mountain. Measurements were taken from the models with a horizontal bar and plumb bob, enlarged twelve times, and transferred to the mountain. After a reference point, such as the tip of a nose, was located, excess rock could be removed with dynamite (some 450,000 tons in all).

Drillers, suspended over the face of the mountain in "swing seats," used jackhammers to honeycomb the surface with shallow holes at intervals of about three inches. The remaining rock was wedged off with a small drill, or a hammer and wedging tool. Finally, the faces were smoothed with small air hammers in a process known as "bumping."

Behind every image is the work of a creator. The four Presidents on Mount Rushmore look remarkably real, though we know it is only rock. They have no life.

So it was with the idols which surround the controversy described in I Corinthians 8. They had been carved by men, but the people had made them into gods and then worshiped them. How absurd that they should bow down to that which they had made with their own hands!

In this context Paul reminds his fellow believers that "to us there is but one God, the Father, of whom are all things, and we [exist] in him" (verse 6). In short, God is the Creator of all, and He owns us. In the same breath he also declares that there is one Lord Jesus Christ, who made everything and gives us life.

Despite the humanism of our day, and the argument over origins, the very existence of man thunders the existence of a Creator. Even the faces on Mount Rushmore could not have simply "evolved" over eons of time as the product of wind, weather, chance and other forces. And man is far more intricate than dead stone. He has life, but only because the Creator has given him life. Where life is, God is. This includes God the Son. "In him was life" (see John 1:4). Only He has the power to grant it (see John 17:2-3).

Man was created in God's image. Ephesians 2:10 expands on this truth: "We are his workmanship, created in Christ Jesus unto good works. . . ."

The Mount Rushmore "Shrine of Democracy."

God has given us eternal life as a free gift, by His grace, but our Christian maturity is a process. Our Lord still has to repair fissures, and chip away the rough spots.

Someday the image will be as God wants it.

More About Stone Faces

Three of the faces on Mount Rushmore—Washington, Jefferson and Roosevelt—cluster together. But Abraham Lincoln alone is off to the side, looking another direction. Some have observed that while three of the Presidents emerged from backgrounds of wealth and aristocracy, Lincoln alone rose from among the humble poor. Those who designed Mount Rushmore would simply explain this interesting arrangement of the men by the fissures in the rock.

At Stone Mountain, Georgia, a monument to the Confederacy, can be seen three more famous figures of history: Robert E. Lee, Stonewall Jackson and Jefferson Davis.

The world's largest man-made sculpture is still in progress. It is the huge 563-foot-high statue of the Sioux chief Crazy Horse, now being blasted out of the rocky face of Thunderbird Mountain not far from Mount Rushmore.

The famous "Great Stone Face" in the mountains of New Hampshire was carved many thousands of years ago not by man, but by nature. Some call this forty-foot granite profile the "old man of the mountains." Years ago Nathaniel Hawthorne gained immortality for the rock formation with his classic short story, "The Great Stone Face"—for which an editor named John Greenleaf Whittier paid him twenty-five dollars. Daniel Webster attributed the work to "God Almighty," who had "hung out a sign to show that there He makes men."

26

What motivates man to heroism?
Does self-interest stand between you and God?

Drama at Sea

Four heroic chaplains gave their lives that others might be saved. Their example helps point to history's Supreme Sacrifice.

Read: Luke 23:33-39

The ***U.S.S. Dorchester***, laden with troops bound for the World War II battlefields, steamed through frigid waters off the coast of Greenland in February, 1943. Suddenly it met the enemy. Germans torpedoed the ship. In a short time it slowly began to sink.

Alarms sounded. Men shouted. One by one, life rafts were lowered

The four chaplains of the **U.S.S. Dorchester.**

over the side, and as men struggled aboard them many hesitated, fearing the icy waters. Amid the turmoil, four chaplains helped the troops abandon ship. They persuaded scores to go overboard, however reluctantly, where there was at least a chance of rescue. (Many were rescued later.)

The four chaplains encouraged the men, prayed with them, helped them into lifeboats and life belts. Finally they gave up their own life jackets. As the bow of the ship sank, men in the water and in lifeboats saw the four chaplains link arms and heard them raise their voices in prayer.

They were still praying together on the deck when the ship made its final plunge.

These men could have tried to save themselves. But they didn't. It was more important to them that others should be saved. Their example of heroism prompted the United States Post Office to release a postage stamp in 1948 that would help the world to remember this drama.

Today's passage from Luke 23 centers on the drama of the Crucifixion. The unruly crowd sneers and shouts, "He saved others; let him save himself. . ." If Jesus was the Christ of God, they said, and indeed the king of the Jews, then let Him prove it.

One of the thieves next to Jesus on the cross, hurling abuse, demanded, "Are you not the Christ? Save yourself and us!" (see verse 39).

But Jesus did not try to save Himself.

He had the power to do so, and Satan would have rejoiced, on this occasion, to see Him use it. Jesus could have saved Himself further pain and agony. But He would have denied God the Father, thwarted the plan of salvation, and played into Satan's hands.

To the crowds that stood by and jeered, it may have seemed that Jesus had lost total control of the situation. Where was the Man who had once healed the sick, raised the dead and stilled the stormy waters of the sea? Does He not now hang helplessly on the cross?

But they had forgotten Jesus' own words, that He was to lay down His life for the sheep: "Therefore doth my Father love me, because I lay down my life, that I might take it again. No man taketh it from me, but I lay it down of myself. I have power to lay it down, and I have power to take it again"(John 10:17-18).

Jesus could have acted from the motive of self-interest and rescued Himself from the cross. But the lives of men and women on planet Earth, including the generations to come, were at stake. Jesus died voluntarily, and suffered the worst of agonies, that you and I might be saved.

Three days later He exercised the right that was His all along. He took back His life, and fulfilled His own promise: "I lay down my life that I might take it again."

"He died for all, that they which live should not henceforth live unto themselves, but unto him which died for them, and rose again" (II Corinthians 5:15).

Suggestion

An old hymn which was set to music by Frances Havergal, is "I Gave My Life For Thee." Think about how you would answer the question found in this hymn.

I gave My life for thee, My precious blood I shed,
That thou might'st ransomed be, And quickened from the dead;
I gave, I gave My life for thee, What hast thou giv'n for Me?
I gave, I gave My life for thee, What hast thou giv'n for Me?

Note:

Military chaplains, or "pastors in uniform," minister in all branches of our armed services. Among the four chaplains on the **U.S.S. Dorchester** were Lieutenant George Fox, a graduate of Chicago's Moody Bible Institute.

Another was the son of Daniel Poling, who for many years published ***The Christian Herald.***

Why do people turn from God?
Are you in need of a personal revival?

27

Early American Camp Meeting

It was an outdoor church in the wilderness—with split logs for pews and tree stumps for pulpits. But it changed the course of a nation.

Read: II Chronicles 7:14

The nation, it seemed, was headed for disaster. It was the late 1700s, and thousands of colonial Americans, until then clustered mostly along the Eastern seaboard, began to pull up roots and head West through the Cumberland Gap.

Conditions at that time did not exactly produce a territory of churchgoers. Once out into the frontier, many left their churches behind. Life became tough and rough. Morals declined.

One writer describes the scene aptly: "Corn liquor flowed freely . . . gun and rope settled far too many legal disputes. The West was crowded with thieves and murderers, with neither courts of law nor public opinion to raise a rebuke." Sexual sin abounded.

Christians who cared about the souls of men and the future of the country saw the peril. If such a spiritual drift should continue among the thousands of settlers already in the Alleghenies and beyond, it could bring down the judgment of God upon the entire young nation.

Yet only a thin system of trails and waterways connected the colonies with that vast wilderness beyond the mountains. Humanly speaking, it seemed impossible for godly men to change the course of events.

But God intervened in a mighty movement now known as the Second Great Awakening. The event surely helped reverse the spiritual skid and saved America from calamity.

Where and when did the great western revival begin?

Most historians pinpoint Kentucky's Logan County about 1799, when several Methodist and Presbyterian preachers joined efforts. Soon word of a mini-revival spread. Kentuckians came from miles around. The crowds grew, and soon visitors had to camp out for one, two or three nights. Men chopped down more trees to accommodate the crowds, and arranged split-log benches to create a church-in-the-wilderness.

A great meeting at Bourbon County's Cane Ridge in August, 1801, climaxed the fervor. It extended over several days and drew crowds estimated as high as 15,000, a remarkable figure in view of the scanty population at that time. The high emotional pitch of the meetings triggered no small controversy, especially among staid clergy of the East. Despite admitted emotional excesses, the revival movement spread and had a profound effect in transforming the lives and morals of western society. Thousands were swept into churches—more than 10,000 in Kentucky alone between 1800 and 1803.

The revival and its impact eventually spread beyond the Kentucky borders, but camp meetings took on more dignity. They became well organized, and the camp meeting established itself as a legitimate Protestant innovation that helped bring the gospel to the masses. Its

Early American camp meeting.

format, in fact, laid the foundations for the later campaigns of mass evangelism that still typify 20th Century evangelicalism.

Revivals both small and great, though generally modest, have continued to sweep segments of the American landscape since those pioneer years. Often God simply renews the spiritual life of a church here and there, or of families, or individuals.

When the people of God no longer seek spiritual renewal, the nation will be in deep trouble. Today's chosen text speaks for itself. The steps for spiritual revival are clear. We must (1) humble ourselves, (2) pray, (3) seek God's face, and (4) turn from any wicked ways.

Our natural bent is to expect the non-believer to turn from his sin. That would be nice, and some may do so, but Scripture speaks first to God's people.

That's where any national revival must begin. Whether in the early days of Israel, on America's early frontier, or in today's time, judgment must always begin in the house of God.

A Camp Meeting Scene

One historian describes this vivid scene of an early camp meeting: "The governor of our State was with us and encouraging the work. They are commonly collected in small circles of ten or twelve, closely adjoining another circle and all engaged in singing Watt's and Hart's hymns: and then a minister steps upon a stump or log, and begins an exhortation or sermon, when as many as can hear collect around him."

Another describes the impressive scene at night: "The glare of camp-fires. . .long ranges of tents. . . hundreds of candles and lamps suspended among the trees. . .the solemn chanting of hymns swelling and falling on the night wind. . . earnest prayers. . .sobs, shrieks, shouts."

It was a time that many families, and especially children, never forgot.

Why do men build walls?
Do you have unnecessary barriers in your life?

Jerusalem in Arkansas?

Walls sometimes appear where you least expect them. They can be welcome. But what can we do about the barriers that unnecessarily divide us?

Read: Ephesians 2:12-18

Tourists traveling the southern Ozarks do a double take these days when they suddenly look up to see the wall of Jerusalem—in the middle of Arkansas!

Sure enough. Even camels linger around the main gate, just like ones you can see today in far-off Old Jerusalem. One may even have a rider on top, dressed as if he had just stepped out of the Bible.

Some years ago a man who wanted Americans to know what the land of the Bible is really like

decided to start building a replica of the Old City of Jerusalem in the Ozarks. It is not a model. He decided to build it to exact size!

One section of the giant five-story wall and the city's main entrance has already been built. The project, when completed, will cost millions of dollars. It is such a huge undertaking that some believe it will never be finished. Only time will tell.

The wall of Jerusalem.

Walls can be fascinating—like the wall of China. They can also be ominous—like the Berlin wall. In the Bible, God helped people like those of Nehemiah's time build great walls. He also brought them down—as in the Battle of Jericho. The great walls of Babylon had once seemed impossible to scale or penetrate. But under cover of darkness the enemy sneaked in through the city's water supply route, and Babylon fell.

In Ephesians 2 Paul talks about the middle wall of partition (verse 14). This was the Temple wall that separated the Court of the Gentiles from the Court of the Jews. Gentiles could not go beyond this wall without facing the death penalty. The wall created Jewish contempt and Gentile resentment.

But when Jesus died on the cross, Paul explains, the feud ended. Now both Jews and Gentiles had access to God, and fellowship with one another. The system of Jewish laws was annulled, and the two peoples could now be fused into one, through faith in Jesus Christ (verse 15).

The judgment of sin upon the world built a wall between man and God. But Jesus Christ, in His death upon the cross, broke through that wall. Sin still builds walls between man and God. But no man upon earth can say now that he can't reach out to God. Jesus is the Way, and He will not refuse those who come to Him.

Christians can still build walls that divide. Do the wrong thing, or say the wrong thing, and you can offend a Christian brother. Suddenly the wall is there. To restore friendship, someone has to break it down.

Walls also often divide races, nationalities, social classes. The highly educated person and the blue-collar worker do not always mix easily.

But in the final analysis, there is no distinction.

Paul makes this clear in Colossians 3:11, a passage that parallels Ephesians 2. A paraphrase puts it in the language of our day: "In this new life one's nationality or race or education or social position is unimportant; such things mean nothing. Whether a person has Christ is what matters, and he is equally available to all."

Walls always crumble at the foot of the cross.

Eureka Springs

The wall of Jerusalem in replica is in the resort town of Eureka Springs in northern Arkansas. This Ozark mountain town is also the site of:

Christ of the Ozarks, a gigantic concrete sculpture of the Saviour with outstretched arms, standing seven stories high on Magnetic Mountain. The statue's armspread from fingertip to fingertip is sixty-five feet. An automobile could be suspended from either wrist without affecting the statue!

The Bible Museum, which contains perhaps the largest number of old Bibles (7,000 volumes) and ancient sacred writings (3,000 primitive manuscripts) ever assembled into a private single collection.

Hatchet Hall, the final home of Carry Nation, who smashed saloons with her hatchet in her early-day crusade against alcohol.

Question

Are there any walls that you need to tear down?

29

A trucker passes some Wandering Wheels climbing the Rocky Mountains.

Is spiritual discipline necessary?
Are you in "top condition" for Christ?

Wandering Wheels

Every year they bike across America. Their grueling trek from coast to coast demands the best in self-discipline. So also does the successful Christian life.

Read: Philippians 3:13-14; 4:11-13

Somewhere, someday, out on the highways of America, you may see them: cross-country bicyclists, as many as sixty of them, traveling in packs of six, from coast to coast.

They usually start with their back tires in the Pacific Ocean and six grueling weeks later they will splash their front tires into the Atlantic.

They're called the Wandering Wheels, a group of Christian young people from colleges across the nation. Students usually join these treks for the rugged self-discipline

the adventure demands of them. Along the way they also encourage those they meet to follow Jesus Christ.

The cyclists have crossed mountain passes higher than 11,000 feet and pedaled into desert temperatures as high as 120 degrees.

The cyclists rise early and, once in stride, they will average as much as 100 miles a day. No matter what the weather, or the conditions, they press on. Discipline is essential.

So it is, also, with the victorious Christian life.

No cross-country bicyclist succeeds with less than full effort. Nor does he even qualify for the adventure without the rigors of pre-conditioning. The task ahead of him will demand all the resources of his body, his mind, his spirit.

So also does the Christian life.

The Apostle Paul describes his own status in Philippians 3:13-14. Despite his spiritual stature, he admits he is not yet in "top condition." But he dare not let his past failures defeat him. Instead, he forgets the past and brings all his energies to bear on that which lies ahead.

It is easy for the Christian to become discouraged with his spiritual progress. Too many wallow in their failures.

It's also possible to become too self-satisfied with past success. A Christian can rest on what he or she has already accomplished for the Lord—perhaps in a church or other Christian organization—and fail to see what is yet to be done. Paul knew he had not yet arrived. The forward look assures that we not let either past success, or past failures,

A coed eases her bike to the edge of the Grand Canyon.

drag us down. It's the territory ahead that deserves our energies.

The passage in Philippians 4 offers further insight both for cross-country bicyclists, and for those conditioning themselves to be Jesus' disciples.

Consider the ability to adjust to new circumstances.

The Wandering Wheels learn quickly what it's like to go without the luxuries of life. They enjoy no built-in air conditioning on a hot day out on the plains, and somehow color television suddenly becomes a non-essential.

Paul seems to be able to handle both prosperity and want. Whether he has much or little does not matter. He has not based his happiness on his possessions. Nor does he let the circumstances around him dictate his mood. At the heart of his joy and confidence is Jesus Christ. That is the source of his strength for whatever may come. "I can do all things through Christ, which strengtheneth me" (4:13). For the Christian, Christ is the secret of contentment in every situation.

The future need not scare you. Like Paul you can look ahead, and press ahead.

But don't forget also to look up.

About the Wandering Wheels

The Wandering Wheels program is sponsored by Indiana's Taylor University, where it originated in 1964 under Taylor coach Bob Davenport, a one-time All American with UCLA. "The real reason I started it," says Davenport, "was to put muscle on the bones of the church; to show teenagers who associate Christianity with mealy-mouthed, milk-toast types that this is not the case."

The cyclists rub shoulders with townspeople along the way, and sleep in gymnasiums and church basements, or out in the open. A front-runner always rides ahead to look for lodging—a good way to trust the Lord on a day-by-day basis.

A van follows the troupe with repair parts and extra tires—which come in handy because the Wandering Wheels average about five flats a day.

One team escorted a blind boy across the United States on a tandem bicycle. Another participated with a young man with only one leg training to cross the United States.

The Wandering Wheels often receive the key of a city they pass through. They have sung to two presidents: Harry Truman and Lyndon Johnson.

30

What does it mean to be spiritually thirsty?
How can you satisfy spiritual thirst?

Water Means Life

Without rainfall, rivers and dams, much of the United States would be a barren wasteland. For souls that thirst, Jesus offers the Water of Life.

Read: John 4:7-14

America's natural resources have helped her to flourish. High on that list of resources has been her supply of water.

Ample year-round rainfall generally waters the East, and at least part of the Midwest. Much of the West is dry, but her citizens have learned to make the most of what water there is. Large dams dot the Western landscape to generate power, water thirsty cities and make the deserts bloom.

On the Colorado River, Boulder Dam—also called Hoover Dam—rises to a height of 726 feet and backs up the waters of gigantic Lake Meade. Built in 1936, it was the tallest dam in the nation until the United States Government completed Oroville Dam on California's Feather River in 1968. It towers 756 feet.

The Coulee Dam, on the Columbia River between Washington and Oregon, gives our nation by far its largest hydroelectric plant. Such dams produce most of the power for the Pacific Northwest.

Even most of California's great Central Valley would be semi-desert were it not for dams and the many rivers which descend from the high Sierras and Cascades. Couple these factors with an intricate system of canals and irrigation lines, and you have the richest agricultural region of the world.

It is water that makes the difference between life on planet Earth, and the barren, lifeless moon. Water covers about seventy percent of the earth's surface. If the surface of the earth were perfectly smooth, the waters of the oceans would cover the earth evenly to a depth of nearly 9,000 feet. Even seventy percent of the human body is water.

Jesus knew that water meant the difference between life and death. It was the perfect analogy for Him to use when He met the Samaritan woman at the well and asked her for a drink (verses 7-9). Once he aroused her curiosity, He offered her ***living*** water, which would quench the longings of her soul and bring her eternal life (verses 10-14).

Only a short time after Jesus had walked on the water, establishing His

Hoover Dam.

Grand Coulee Dam.

authority over Creation, He used the analogy again. "He who believes in me shall never thirst" (John 6:35b).

Later He said to the crowds, "If any man is thirsty, let him come to Me and drink" (John 7:37b, NASB). He used water, in this context, to describe the qualities of the Holy Spirit.

And in the closing chapter of the Bible—even in the closing verses—an angel conveys to John on the isle of Patmos this message from the risen Christ: "Let the one who is thirsty come; let the one who wishes take the water of life without cost" (Revelation 22:17b, NASB).

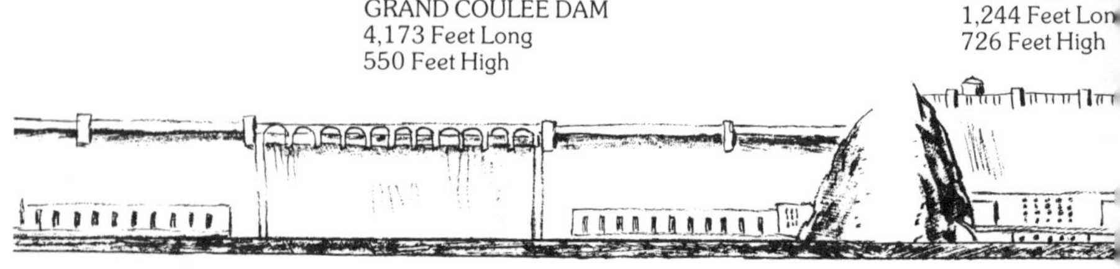

It is the only answer for the spiritually dry or thirsty soul.

Our Water Cycle

Earth's constant "water cycle" waters the land and sustains life. The heat of the sun evaporates water into the sky from oceans, lakes and rivers. It rises because warm "wet" air is lighter than cold "dry" air. Clouds form from warm moist air. Prevailing winds send the moisture up steep mountain slopes, where it cools and condenses. Its effect is to "squeeze out" the moisture, so it falls as refreshing rain. The waters drain once more toward lakes, rivers and oceans.

Science calls this the "hydrological cycle." Yet three thousand years before these principles were discovered by modern science, the Bible described the water cycle with amazing accuracy: "All the rivers run into the sea; yet the sea is not full; unto the place from whence the rivers come, thither they return again" (Ecclesiastes 1:7).

De-salting Sea Water

Man has long tried to remove salt from sea water to produce water for drinking and irrigation. The process is called "desalination." Huge plants have been built near some of the world's coastlines to convert sea water to fresh water. But despite the advances of modern science, it is still an extremely expensive process.

Yet, from the very beginning, God has converted billions of tons of salt water to fresh—every day!

(Note: For a fascinating glimpse of water on planet Earth, the author recommends the film, "Where the Waters Run," produced by the Moody Institute of Science.)

Water blesses our land, but it costs to harness it and to utilize it. Americans pay taxes to build federal dams. Farmers pay irrigation fees. Homeowners pay their water bills. But the Water of Life is without charge.

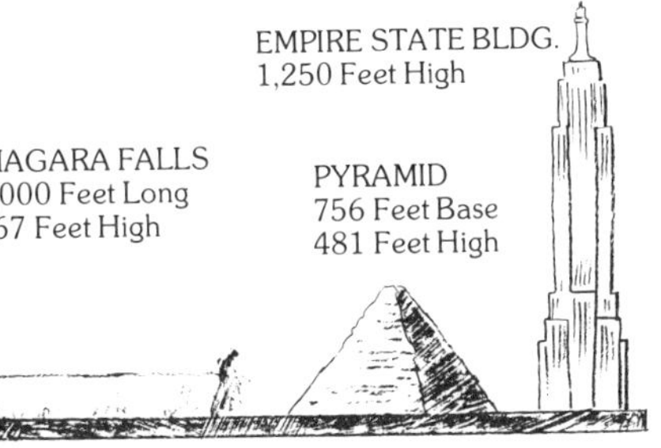

31

Should Christian views be represented in our government? How can you make a difference?

Journey of an Atheist

In 1963 Madalyn Murray O'Hair and her son, Billy, won an historic Supreme Court decision. Why now does Bill Murray want to change it?

Read: Romans 1:19-21

On June 17,1963, the Supreme Court of the United States issued an historic decision. It ruled 8-1 in favor of a lawsuit filed by atheist Madalyn Murray and her son, Billy, then 17. School-sponsored prayer and Bible reading would have to be expelled from public school classrooms. In fear of further lawsuits, many other schools went even further, and banned before-school and after-school Bible clubs.

Billy had helped his mother file the lawsuit. He also helped her staple, fold and mail her monthly atheist newsletter. For years William Murray continued to work for atheistic causes.

Then on January 24, 1980, in San Francisco, a disturbing dream prompted him to climb out of bed and search out a Bible at an all-night discount store. Back in his San Francisco apartment, he eagerly devoured the Gospel of Luke. That night he invited Jesus into his life.

The change in his life was dramatic. Where he had once seethed with hate, he felt love. A few weeks later he wrote a letter to the ***Baltimore Sun.*** It read in part: ". . . I would like to apologize to the people of the City of Baltimore for whatever part I played in the removal of Bible reading and praying from the public schools of that city. . . . Being raised as an atheist in the home of Madalyn O'Hair, I was not aware of faith or even the existence of God. As I now look back over 33 years of life wasted without faith in God, I pray only that I can, with His help, right some of the wrong and evil I have caused. . . ."

In April, 1982, William Murray and several others delivered to the White House petitions bearing the signatures of one million Americans who want freedom for voluntary prayer in public schools.

Only a tiny percentage of Americans call themselves atheists, which means they believe there is no God. Others prefer to refer to themselves as "agnostics." These people say there ***may*** be a God, but we don't know.

Romans 1:19-20 speaks to the issue. The world around us—the earth and the sky and all creation—shouts the existence of God. Every man has an instinctive awareness of God, though he can allow himself to be brainwashed until he thinks otherwise. Yet though he may never have read the Bible, or gone to church, God says he is without excuse (verse 20). The evidence of God's existence surrounds him.

What a person believes about God, or does not believe, sooner or later will dictate his actions. The verses of Romans 1 which follow verse 21 describe the kind of degradation into which the denial of God can eventually lead.

Whenever man rejects God, he falls for a counterfeit. Communism, for instance, rejects God, and then makes the State supreme. This means the Communist can justify any act he wants, including mass murder, if it's for the "good of the State."

In the final analysis, say the Scriptures, the atheist emerges as "a fool." The opening verse both of Psalm 14 and Psalm 53 says it succinctly: "The fool hath said in his heart, There is no God."

Note:

William Murray's letter of apology to the ***Baltimore Sun*** created a storm of publicity, and articles soon appeared in ***Time*** and ***People*** magazines. Since then William Murray has formed a Christian foundation and crisscrossed the country warning people of the dangers of atheism. His full story is told in the book, ***My Life Without God,*** released by Thomas Nelson Publishers.

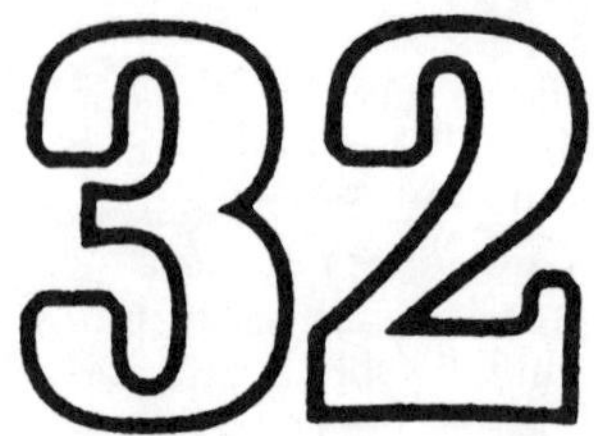

Can freedom be abused?
Do Christians have special responsibilities to America?

A Patriot's Hymn of Liberty and Law

The blessings of freedom do not mean we are free to do wrong.

Read: I Peter 2:13-17

In 1893 a New England schoolteacher went West to spend a summer in Colorado Springs. One day, with a party of friends, she climbed into a "prairie wagon" for an outing on nearby Pike's Peak. The wagon slowly made its way to the top of the 14,110-foot mountain, where Katherine Lee Bates looked out for miles in every direction.

It seemed to her as if she were standing on the roof of the world. Great ridges and valleys stretched away to the north and west, and the plains to the east reached out toward the state of Kansas.

Because of the thin air the group did not remain at the top long but it was long enough for Katherine to write a poem. The words were later set to music by Samuel A. Ward. The song became one of America's greatest patriotic hymns:

O beautiful for spacious skies,
For amber waves of grain,
For purple mountain majesties
Above the fruited plain
America, America, God shed
His grace on thee. . .

Some people criticize patriotism. They seem to feel such emotions foster a blind allegiance to all America does, right or wrong. Such critics misread the meaning of patriotism, in its purest sense. The true patriot loves his country dearly, but he does not ignore wrongs, nor the chance to correct them. In fact, he wants to see wrongs remedied precisely because he loves his country so much!

The lyrics that Katherine Bates wrote recognize this. They plead that God "mend the country's every flaw." They ask that the people not abuse their liberties.

Confirm thy soul in self control,
Thy liberty in law.

Today's Scripture passage reminds us that we are to obey the laws of our government. This still leaves room for some healthy criticism, if it's needed, and along with this the latitude to right wrongs. But the privileges of liberty always demand a sense of brotherhood, and a climate of law and order. Nor dare we abuse the freedom we enjoy. To do so can only undermine the very freedoms, and also undercut the meaning for genuine reform.

There's a parallel here for the born-again Christian who enjoys special freedoms in Jesus Christ. The Book of Romans talks much about these freedoms, but also warns that such freedom from the law, which gives us salvation by grace alone, must not be abused. Should the Christian sin simply because God's grace abounds? "God forbid" (see Romans 7).

When God sheds His grace, either on a nation or on an individual, there is always a danger that some people will use such liberties to actually flout the laws of God. Let's not minimize our freedoms, but neither let us abuse them.

Nations must exercise self-control, and so must every Christian. The grace of God still demands that we exercise self-discipline. Many are shouting today for their "rights," of one kind or another. Some rights are legitimate, but liberty never gives anyone the right to do wrong.

Questions

What link do you see between physical discipline of the body and spiritual discipline?

What are some of the ways in which God has "shed His grace" on America?

Chronology of events in this book

- ☐ 1620 Pilgrims land at Plymouth Rock.
- ☐ 1646 The Puritans establish Harvard.
- ☐ 1670 William Penn acquires what later becomes the state of Pennsylvania and the state of Delaware.
- ☐ 1701 Yale is founded by Christians.
- ☐ 1716 The "Boston Light," first U.S. lighthouse, is erected.
- ☐ 1771 Circuit rider-to-be Francis Asbury sails for America.
- ☐ 1783 Treaty with England gives U.S. almost everything east of the Mississippi.
- ☐ 1801 Revival meeting at Cane Ridge in Kentucky wilderness draws thousands.
- ☐ 1803 U.S. doubles its size with the Louisiana Purchase.
- ☐ 1814 Francis Scott Key pens ***The Star Spangled Banner*** during the Battle of Baltimore.
- ☐ 1816 Circuit rider Francis Asbury dies after more than forty years of roaming the American wilderness.
- ☐ 1819 U.S. purchases Florida from Spain.
- ☐ 1828 Noah Webster completes his ***American Dictionary.***
- ☐ 1828 Yale students evangelize Illinois and become known as the "Illinois Band."
- ☐ 1842 Thousands begin to migrate West over the Oregon Trail.
- ☐ 1844 Samuel F. B. Morse sends the first telegraph message, "What hath God wrought."
- ☐ 1845 U.S. buys from Spain what is now much of Texas and New Mexico.
- ☐ 1846 U.S. acquires the Oregon Territory.
- ☐ 1847 Marcus and Narcissa Whitman and other missionaries are murdered by the Indians at Walla Walla.
- ☐ 1848 Treaty with Mexico gives U.S. several western states, including California.

- ☐ 1848 Gold discovered at California's Sutter's Creek.
- ☐ 1853 Gadsden Purchase adds territory near Mexican border.
- ☐ 1860 The Pony Express is launched.
- ☐ 1861 Abraham Lincoln becomes the 16th President of the United States.
- ☐ 1873 San Francisco gets its first cable railroad.
- ☐ 1880 James Garfield becomes the 20th President of the United States.
- ☐ 1893 Katherine Lee Bates pens the lyrics of "America, the Beautiful" atop Pike's Peak.
- ☐ 1930 ***The Star Spangled Banner*** is adopted as the U.S. national anthem.
- ☐ 1931 Nashville builds a replica of the Greek Parthenon.
- ☐ 1932 J. C. Penney goes broke from the stock market crash.
- ☐ 1936 U.S. Government completes Hoover Dam.
- ☐ 1939 The "Shrine of Democracy" at Mt. Rushmore, South Dakota, is completed.
- ☐ 1941 The Japanese, led by Mitsuo Fuchida, bomb Pearl Harbor.
- ☐ 1943 George Washington Carver, who found more than 300 uses for the peanut, dies.
- ☐ 1943 Germans sink the U.S.S. Dorchester off the coast of Iceland.
- ☐ 1963 Historic Supreme Court decision outlaws prayer in the public schools.
- ☐ 1964 Christian coach Bob Davenport organizes "The Wandering Wheels."
- ☐ 1968 Apollo 8 astronauts orbit the moon and read from the Book of Genesis.
- ☐ 1968 U.S. Government completes Oroville Dam, tallest in the U.S.
- ☐ 1971 Apollo 15 lands on the moon.
- ☐ 1980 Mt. St. Helens erupts in Washington state.
- ☐ 1980 The son of atheist Madalyn Murray O'Hair is converted.
- ☐ 1982 Astronaut Jack Lousma flies space shuttle Columbia.

Photo Credits

Page	
16	National Aeronautics and Space Administration
21	Maine Publicity Bureau
26	Knott's Berry Farm
34-35	Division of Travel and Tourism, Lincoln, Nebraska
36	National Park Service
56	Missouri Division of Tourism
58	*Peninsula Times-Tribune*
63	Washington State Division of Tourism
64	Wyoming Travel Commission
72-73	S. Joe McKenzie
83	Taylor University, Upland, Indiana
84-85	Taylor University, Upland, Indiana